Travel Medicine

Handbook of

Travel Medicine

Yvonne Ganley

Liverpool School of Tropical Medicine
Liverpool, UK

SCIENCE PRESS

Published by Science Press Ltd., 34–42 Cleveland St., London W1P 6LB, UK.

British Library Cataloguing in Publication Data
A catalogue record for this book is available from the British Library

ISBN 1-85873-120-8

This copy of *Handbook of Travel Medicine* is given as a service to medicine by SmithKline Beecham. Sponsorship of this copy does not imply the sponsor's agreement or otherwise with the views expressed herein.

Although every effort has been made to ensure that drug doses and other information are presented accurately in this publication, the ultimate responsibility rests with the prescribing physician. Neither the publishers nor the authors can be held responsible for errors or for any consequences arising from the use of the information contained herein. Any product mentioned in this publication should be used in accordance with the prescribing information prepared by the manufacturers. No claims or endorsements are made for any drug or compound at present under clinical investigation.

Project editor: Hilary Dean
Illustrator: Matthew McCutcheon
Typesetter: Simon Banister
Cover design: Claire Huntley
Production: Kate Oldfield
Printed in Spain

10 9 8 7 6 5 4 3 2 1

CONTENTS

Acknowledgements **vi**

1 Introduction **1**
- 1.1 Personal protection for the traveller 1
- 1.2 Risk assessment 1

Before travel

2 Vaccination and the traveller **3**
- 2.1 Vaccination schedules 3
- 2.2 Contraindications to routine vaccination 4
- 2.3 Live vaccines: guidelines for use 5
- 2.4 HIV-positive travellers and vaccination 5
- 2.5 Claiming for vaccinations 6

3 Malaria and the traveller **7**
- 3.1 Malaria: the disease 7
- 3.2 Malaria prevention 9
- 3.3 Special cases and malaria 14
- 3.4 Standby treatment 15

4 Special cases and travel **17**
- 4.1 Pregnant women 17
- 4.2 Children 18
- 4.3 Former immigrants and visitors from developing countries 20
- 4.4 Travellers with pre-existing health problems 21

While away

5 Staying healthy abroad **23**
- 5.1 First-aid kits 23
- 5.2 Diarrhoea 24
- 5.3 Sexually transmitted disease and contraception 25
- 5.4 Accidents 28
- 5.5 Sun 28
- 5.6 Insects, worms and other animals 29
- 5.7 Flying 30

On return

6 The returned traveller **32**
- 6.1 Malaria prevention: continuing prophylaxis 32
- 6.2 Illness in the returned traveller 32
- 6.3 Screening the asymptomatic returned traveller 33

Appendices

- **I Country guidelines** **34**
- **II Vaccine guidelines** **60**
- **III Further study** **86**
- **IV Useful addresses** **87**
- **V Information for travellers** **88**

Index **89**

ACKNOWLEDGEMENTS

Many thanks are due to Dr George Wyatt for his comments and contributions and to Isobel Allen and Dr Emma Woolfenden who contributed to the text. I am also grateful to all the staff at the Liverpool School of Tropical Medicine who gave encouragement and support. Thank you as well to Hilary Dean and her colleagues at Science Press for their help in preparing the book.

The recommendations for vaccines and malaria prophylaxis were agreed by consultants in tropical medicine at the Liverpool School of Tropical Medicine. I would like to acknowledge the World Health Organization (WHO) which gave kind permission to use their maps and information about malaria and other disease risks.

Page 8

Adapted with permission from WHO: *Weekly Epidemiological Record* 1996, **71**:37.

Page 26

Adapted with permission from WHO: *Weekly Epidemiological Record* 1995, **27**:196.

Page 67

Adapted with permission from WHO: *Expanded Programme on Immunization: Update* 1989.

Page 69–70

Adapted with permission from US Centers for Disease Control and Prevention: **Risk of Japanese encephalitis by country, region and season**. In *Morbidity and Mortality Weekly Report, Recommendations and Reports 1993*, Vol 42, No. RR-1.

Page 70

Adapted with permission from WHO: *Weekly Epidemiological Record* 1994 **16**:114.

Page 74

Adapted with permission from WHO: *Weekly Epidemiological Record* 1995 **14**:99.

Page 85

Adapted with permission from WHO: *International Travel and Health. Vaccination Requirements and Health Advice* 1996:14–15.

1 INTRODUCTION

1.1 Personal protection for the traveller

Health problems are common in travellers, especially in those spending time in developing countries. Accidents and cardiovascular disease are the leading causes of death. Deaths during travel to less developed countries due to injuries are two- to threefold higher in the 15–44 year age group than in the same age group at home (in industrialized countries) [Hargarten *et al.*, *Ann Emerg Med* 1991, **20**:622–626]. Malaria is a significant problem; in the UK, about 2000 cases are reported each year, with up to 10 deaths. HIV infection is also a serious hazard. Diarrhoeal disease is the most common health problem in travellers. Vaccines can prevent only a minority of travel health problems, but they do protect against some infections that have a high incidence of morbidity or mortality.

Awareness of risk and knowledge of preventive measures are important if problems are to be avoided. With increasing numbers of people travelling to remote and unusual destinations, pre-travel health questions from the general public are more frequent and more complex because of the nature of travel and the increasing awareness of risk. In this book, I have tried to answer many of the pre-travel questions that are frequently asked, focusing on vaccines and malaria prophylaxis. Other general health risks should also be discussed with travellers.

Advice for travellers

Make sure that medical insurance is sufficient to cover repatriation

Use appropriate malaria prevention and protection against insect bites

Make sure that you have the appropriate vaccines

Follow good food and water hygiene

Take appropriate precautions to avoid accidents

Avoid sexually transmitted diseases

1.2 Risk assessment

The risk involved for any individual depends on several factors, including the destination, mode of travel and length of stay. Travellers should be asked about their exact itinerary and circumstances of travel: a backpacker travelling through Asia for several months will be at a higher risk than a business executive staying in a first-class hotel for a few days.

High-risk groups

Travellers belonging to high-risk groups should be seen as long before travel as possible so that vaccine courses can be completed and to allow time for potential problems to be addressed.

High-risk groups include:

- Former immigrants and visitors from developing countries
- Travellers with pre-existing health problems
- Travellers living in developing countries for long periods
- Pregnant women
- Children

See Special cases and travel.

Information required from travellers

Countries to be visited

Type of travel and accommodation

Length of stay

Time of year

What locality they are visiting, and whether they are travelling in rural or urban areas

Type of employment while away

How much time is available before departure*

Age, health and previous medical and vaccination history

Contraindications to vaccinations and specific malaria prophylaxis

*Travellers should be advised to attend for vaccines and advice well in advance of travel, particularly if visiting malarious areas or if the trip will last more than 1 month. Last-minute bookings are frequent but can cause difficulties in provision of adequate protection. In this situation, as much advice and protection as possible should be given, including malaria prophylaxis.

2 VACCINATION AND THE TRAVELLER

Some travellers' health problems can be prevented by vaccination. Vaccines confer protection against certain infectious diseases, although the degree of protection depends on the vaccine and the individual.

Advice about protection from rare but potentially fatal diseases, such as Japanese encephalitis, is difficult to give. Vaccination for the average tourist may not be appropriate, but for long-term residents or high-risk groups, vaccination is likely to be beneficial (*see Special cases and travel*).

2.1 Vaccination schedules

Types of vaccines

Vaccines can be of the live or killed type.

Live vaccines: contain attenuated live organisms, which are good at stimulating an immune response but can be dangerous in people with impaired immunity; the current live vaccines are oral polio (poliomyelitis), yellow fever, oral typhoid, BCG (bacille Calmette–Guérin), measles and MMR (measles–mumps–rubella)

Killed or inactivated vaccines: contain only material that is dead and cannot replicate in the body; several doses must usually be given to produce an adequate immune response

Human normal immunoglobulin contains antibodies against hepatitis A and is sometimes given to provide immediate short-term protection against hepatitis A. It is not a vaccine.

Schedules

- Interrupted or incomplete courses of vaccination should not be restarted. The course of the vaccination should be continued with the remaining doses given at the recommended intervals. However, if an individual has only received a single dose of oral polio or diphtheria–tetanus in their lifetime, and this was given several years earlier, a full primary course is recommended
- The recommended interval between doses should be followed when possible
- Several vaccines can be given at the same time, at different sites. This is often more convenient and simplifies schedules; adverse effects are rare. However, if a reaction does occur, identifying the cause can be difficult
- Special attention should be paid with live vaccines. These should be given on the same day as other live vaccines, or at least 3 weeks apart. Oral polio and oral typhoid vaccines should not be given at the same time because of possible interference in the gut; a gap of at least 2 weeks is advised
- Human normal immunoglobulin, used for hepatitis A protection, can be given at the same time as yellow fever, oral typhoid and oral polio booster vaccines. It does not inhibit the effect of yellow fever or oral typhoid vaccines and, when oral polio is being given as a booster dose, the effect is not likely to be significant

- To encourage compliance, schedules should be kept simple, with as few visits for vaccination as possible
- Booster doses should usually only be given if risk continues

See Vaccine guidelines (Appendix II).

Routes of administration

Most vaccines are given either by deep subcutaneous or intramuscular injection.

Intradermal injection is recommended for some vaccines. Correct technique must be used. Information about the technique is available in the literature *(see Immunisation against Infectious Diseases [Appendix III]*).

See Vaccine guidelines (Appendix II).

2.2 Contraindications to routine vaccination

Contraindications to routine administration of all vaccines include:

- Acute febrile illness: the vaccination should be postponed
- Severe local or general reaction to a previous dose of the same vaccine
  Local: extensive area of redness and swelling that becomes indurated and involves most of the anterolateral surface of the thigh or a major part of the circumference of the upper arm
  General: fever of at least 39.5°C within 48 h of the vaccine; anaphylaxis, bronchospasm, laryngeal oedema. Prolonged unresponsiveness; prolonged screaming for more than 4 h; convulsions or encephalopathy within 72 h

Special cases to be considered include:

- Contraindications to live vaccines: *see Live vaccines: guidelines for use*
- Pregnancy: *see Pregnancy*
- Allergies: vaccines contain various products that cause allergic reactions in a few people; for example, penicillin is present in trace amounts in both polio vaccines. Previous anaphylactic reaction to egg is a contraindication to yellow fever and MMR vaccines. Check the product information for the contents of each vaccine
- Immunosuppression due to disease or treatment: live vaccines should not be given to immunosuppressed patients. Inactivated vaccines can be given safely to such people but they may have a less than optimal immune response. Hepatitis A vaccine is likely to be effective in patients with mild immunosuppression, but immunoglobulin is preferable for patients with severe immunosuppression
- HIV-positive travellers: special consideration is required and a doctor should be consulted
- Tetanus–diphtheria or tetanus vaccine: avoid over-immunization as hypersensitivity reactions may occur if too many doses are given

See Vaccine guidelines (Appendix II).

Guidelines for referral

The following groups of patients should be discussed with a doctor before vaccination:

- Pregnant women
- HIV-positive individuals
- Travellers with possible contraindications to live vaccines
- Any traveller about whom you feel unsure

2.3 Live vaccines: guidelines for use

Live vaccines must be used with care and should be avoided in the following patients:

- Patients taking corticosteroids: a doctor should be consulted; live vaccines should not be given to patients receiving high doses of corticosteroids and for at least 3 months after stopping treatment
- Patients receiving other forms of immunosuppressive therapy, radiation or chemotherapy: at least 6 months should elapse after cessation of therapy before receiving vaccination with a live virus
- Patients suffering from lymphomas, leukaemia, Hodgkin's disease or other tumours of the reticuloendothelial system
- Patients known to have an impaired immune response, such as hypogammaglobulinaemia
- Pregnant women, except in special circumstances

Special guidelines exist for live vaccine use in HIV-positive travellers.

See Vaccine guidelines (Appendix II).

2.4 HIV-positive travellers and vaccination

Live vaccines

Polio: oral polio vaccine can be given to asymptomatic individuals, who should be warned that faecal excretion of the virus may continue for longer than in normal individuals (more than 6 weeks); symptomatic individuals should be given the inactivated polio vaccine

Oral typhoid: this should not be given; the polysaccharide typhoid vaccine can be used instead

Yellow fever: both the vaccine and travel to high-risk areas should be avoided if possible, though the vaccine is probably safe in those with a CD4 count $> 500 \times 10^6$/l. If a yellow fever certificate is required for entry, an exemption certificate can be given; for unavoidable travel to high-risk areas, vaccination of asymptomatic individuals is warranted and a specialist should be consulted

BCG: this should not be given

Inactivated vaccines

HIV-positive travellers, symptomatic or asymptomatic, can receive all standard inactivated vaccines, but a specialist should be consulted because the immune response to vaccination is usually lower. When protection against hepatitis A is advised, immunoglobulin is preferable to hepatitis A vaccine in those patients with significant immunosuppression.

2.5 Claiming for vaccinations

A simplified version of the rules follows, but the precise guidelines vary depending on the Family Health Service Authority or Health Board. Currently, general practitioners can be reimbursed for administering the following travel vaccines:

- Hepatitis A (or human normal immunoglobulin)
- Injectable typhoid (typhoid vaccine or the polysaccharide typhoid vaccine)
- Hepatitis B and meningococcal A&C: when it is given to certain 'at-risk' travellers
- Polio: when given for travel to areas where polio is endemic (or has been endemic until recently)
- Tetanus: not specifically for travel but, if vaccination would normally be recommended as a 'routine' booster, cost will be reimbursed

For detailed information consult government guidelines (see The Red Book [Appendix III]) and consult your Family Health Service Authority or Health Board.

3 MALARIA AND THE TRAVELLER

3.1 Malaria: the disease

How is it caught? Malaria is a protozoal infection caught from the bite of an infected mosquito. These mosquitoes bite mainly between sunrise and sunset. Malaria is not contagious

What are the different types of malaria? Malaria is caused by four species of *Plasmodium: P. falciparum, P. vivax, P. ovale* and *P. malariae*. Falciparum malaria (sometimes called cerebral or malignant malaria) causes almost all deaths from malaria. Malaria can occur several years after exposure, although falciparum malaria usually manifests within 3 months. Falciparum malaria occurs in many malarious areas and is particularly common in sub-Saharan Africa, where each year it causes the deaths of about 1 million children aged less than 5 years

Is there a vaccine? No. Vaccine trials are in progress, but an effective vaccine has not yet been found

Who gets malaria? Anyone. Most people who grow up in areas with much malaria gradually develop some immunity over many years as a result of continual or frequent exposure to infection. Immunity is rapidly lost during periods spent in non-malarious areas. Expatriates do not develop immunity and thus must take prophylaxis for the duration of their stay when living in endemic areas for long periods

Where are the risk areas? Malaria is present in many parts of the world *(see map)*

What are the symptoms? Symptoms of malaria are non-specific; many people complain of an influenza-like illness with fever and symptoms such as headache, generalized aching, shivering or diarrhoea. With falciparum malaria, rapid deterioration can then occur, with general organ failure affecting the brain and other organs. Symptoms of deterioration are varied but often include clouding of consciousness and confusion. Death from malaria in non-immune people can occur very rapidly (sometimes within 1–2 days; especially in children)

How is malaria diagnosed? The only reliable method of diagnosis is by examination of a blood film (*see Malaria prevention: continuing prophylaxis*); a specialist should be consulted. Remember to enquire about recent travel and consider malaria in patients presenting with fever or influenza-like symptoms.

Can all malaria be prevented? No, but the risk of catching the disease can be greatly reduced by prevention of bites and prophylaxis. However, no prophylaxis is 100% effective

Malaria incidence

Every year, about 2000 cases of malaria are reported in the UK, with 6–10 deaths. Deaths are almost exclusively due to falciparum malaria and could generally be prevented by early diagnosis and adequate treatment. In 1992–1993, 14 people died from falciparum malaria, 12 of whom contracted the disease in Africa and two in India. Eight of these had taken no prophylaxis. More than one-third of malaria cases were in former immigrants who returned to their country of origin to visit relatives and friends [Bradley *et al.*, *Comm Dis Rep* 1994, **4**:R13].

Epidemiological assessment of the status of malaria, 1993

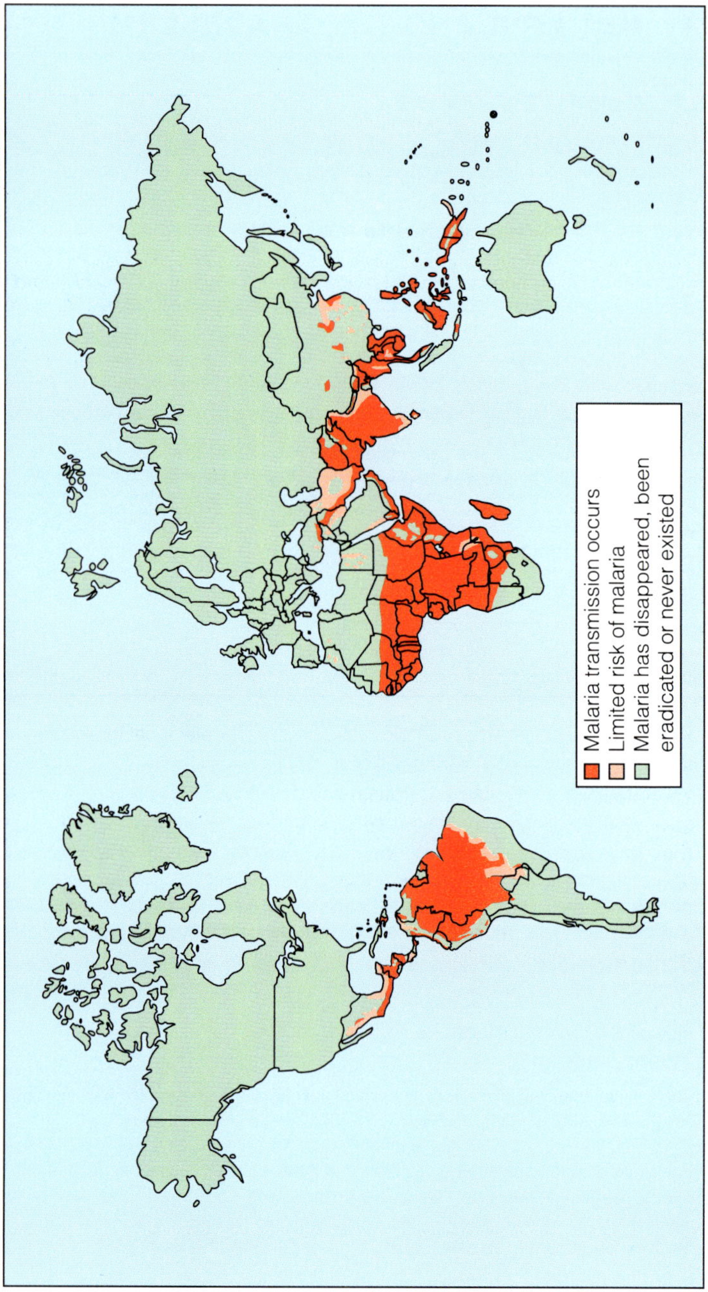

Advice for travellers

Be aware of the risk

Avoid mosquito bites

Take the appropriate antimalarials for the correct length of time

Seek medical help promptly if a fever or influenza-like symptoms occur — no antimalarials are 100% effective

The World Health Organization estimates about 16 000 imported cases annually in Europe, with 300–500 million cases worldwide. More than 90% of these cases originate from countries in tropical Africa [*Weekly Epidemiological Record* 1996, **71**(3):18; **71**(6):47].

3.2 Malaria prevention

Avoiding bites

The mosquitoes that carry malaria bite from dusk until dawn; bite avoidance is most important during these hours.

Advice for travellers

Sleep in a screened or air-conditioned room and kill mosquitoes already in the room with a knock-down pyrethrum spray

Use a mosquito net (especially in less protected accommodation); impregnating the net with permethrin makes it much more effective; permethrin-impregnated lightweight nets and permethrin kits are widely available in the UK

Repel mosquitoes with pyrethroid mosquito coils or electrical insecticide dispensers that contain tablets impregnated with pyrethroids

Wear long-sleeved shirts and trousers after dusk

Use repellents containing diethyl-toluamide (DEET) or a eucalyptus-based repellent (Mosiguard Natural); DEET should be used only on the clothing of children aged less than 5 years, not directly on their skin; alternatively, Mosiguard Natural can be used directly on the skin. Repellents are available in various forms including sprays and gels; ankle and wrist bands soaked with DEET are also available

Most items above can be bought from camping shops, chemists and travel clinics. Electronic buzzers are not effective.

Prophylaxis

The increase in drug resistance in specific areas and the side effects of the drugs have made choosing the correct prophylaxis regimens more difficult. The risk of malaria in the countries of destination must be known; this may vary according to the area visited.

See Country guidelines (Appendix I).

No prophylaxis is 100% effective. Advice about anti-mosquito measures is important, as is advice to seek medical help if a fever or influenza-like symptoms occur 7 days or more after arriving in a malarious area or within 1–2 years of return.

Information required from travellers

When choosing a suitable regimen, various factors must be taken into account:

What countries and localities are being visited: when a person is travelling to more than one destination, one regimen is preferred for the whole period of travel to encourage compliance

When travelling, length of stay and type of accommodation

Known drug sensitivity

Also find out about:

Previous reactions to prophylaxis

History of psychiatric disorder, including depression or anxiety

Personal or family history of fits or convulsions

History of heart, kidney or liver problems

History of psoriasis

Pregnancy or possible pregnancy and breast feeding

Current medication

Advice for travellers

Follow instructions for taking medication: compliance is essential

Start antimalarials 1 week before travel (2–3 weeks for mefloquine) and continue for 4 weeks after leaving the malarious area: most malarial infections are prevented using this regimen

Take antimalarials after meals to minimize the risk of minor side effects

Do not stop antimalarials if minor side effects occur, but seek medical advice if symptoms persist

If serious side effects occur, stop taking the antimalarials and change to another regimen (usually the second-choice regimen for the area)

Prescription of prophylaxis

The Department of Health states that prophylactic antimalarial medication should be prescribed privately. Mefloquine and doxycycline can be prescribed privately. Chloroquine and proguanil are available directly from pharmacists.

Drugs for prophylaxis

Common side effects and contraindications only are given for each drug. For more detailed information refer to recommended guidelines (see British National Formulary [Appendix III]).

For first- and second-choice prophylaxis in individual areas see Country guidelines (Appendix I). The recommendations for prophylaxis given are in accordance with the British guidelines and information supplied by the World Health Organization.

Recent controversy has centred around the use of mefloquine. Some of the important factors to consider when advising travellers about prophylaxis are listed below.

Risk of catching malaria: particularly in areas with high malaria risk and highly chloroquine-resistant malaria, the frequency of adverse reactions to prophylaxis must be balanced against the risk of severe malaria illness and death from falciparum malaria

Effectiveness of prophylaxis: mefloquine is a highly protective prophylaxis. In sub-Saharan Africa, it is considerably more effective than the combination of chloroquine and proguanil (East Africa, prophylactic effectiveness mefloquine 91%, chloroquine plus proguanil 72% [Steffen *et al., Lancet* 1993, **341**:1299–1303])

Adverse reactions to prophylaxis: mefloquine is probably associated with a greater frequency of neuropsychiatric adverse effects than chloroquine and proguanil, but considerable variation exists between studies. The overall frequency of adverse reactions with mefloquine, regardless of type and severity, was 19% [Steffen *et al.*, *Lancet* 1993, **341**:1299–1303]

The risk of adverse reactions to mefloquine is greatest with the early doses, decreasing with subsequent doses

Other factors: contraindications to a particular prophylaxis; duration of visit and type of travel; the importance of compliance with prophylaxis and avoidance of mosquito bites must be stressed

CHLOROQUINE	
Use	Alone in areas with no chloroquine resistance; also in combination with proguanil *(see below)*
Adult dosage	300 mg base weekly
Length of prophylaxis	Start 1 week before travel and continue until 4 full weeks after leaving the malarious area
Children	Safe at correct dosage *(see Children)*
Pregnancy	Can be taken *(see Pregnant women)*
Breast-feeding	Can be taken
Contraindications	Epilepsy (mildly epileptogenic); renal impairment *(see Special cases and malaria)*
Side effects	Nausea, diarrhoea, itching, blurred vision; psoriasis may worsen; rarely blood disorders, psychosis
Long-term use	Chloroquine can be taken for up to 5 years at the prophylactic dose; retinal damage is extremely rare on 300 mg a week dosage but is a hazard if high doses are used

PROGUANIL	
Use	Alone in areas with no chloroquine resistance, if chloroquine is contraindicated; also in combination with chloroquine *(see below)*
Adult dosage	200 mg daily
Length of prophylaxis	Start 1 week before travel and continue until 4 full weeks after leaving the malarious area
Children	Safe at correct dosage *(see Children)*
Pregnancy	Can be taken; folic acid supplements (5 mg daily or on alternate days) should be taken *(see Pregnant women)*
Breast-feeding	Can be taken
Contraindications	Proguanil may potentiate the effect of warfarin; if taking anticoagulants, the anticoagulant dose should be restabilized before travel; renal impairment *(see Special cases and malaria)*
Side effects	Mouth ulceration (folic acid may be beneficial), gastric upsets
Long-term use	Can be taken indefinitely

NOTE: **CHLOROQUINE PLUS PROGUANIL** can be used in areas with moderate chloroquine-resistant falciparum malaria and in travellers unable to take mefloquine who are travelling to sub-Saharan Africa or the Amazon basin region, where the combination is reasonably effective; combine with good anti-mosquito protection

MEFLOQUINE

Use	First-choice drug in areas where resistance to chloroquine and proguanil is widespread
Adult dosage	250 mg weekly
Length of prophylaxis	Start 2–3 weeks before travel and continue until 4 full weeks after leaving the malarious area
Children	Not recommended for children weighing less than 15 kg
Pregnancy	Avoid in first 3 months of pregnancy. Inadvertent pregnancy while taking mefloquine prophylaxis is not considered an indication for termination; a specialist should be consulted *(see Pregnant women)*
Breast-feeding	Avoid
Contraindications	History of epilepsy (and epilepsy in a first-degree relative) or of a psychiatric disorder (including psychosis and depression); severe liver impairment; pilots (and others who undertake precision activities); women in the first trimester of pregnancy; women who may become pregnant within 3 months of stopping the drug. Care should be taken with patients taking beta blockers because current experience is insufficient to rule out the possibility of interactions
Side effects	Nausea, bad dreams and headaches; less frequently psychiatric side effects such as anxiety, depression, psychosis and hallucinations; may also cause dizziness, poor memory and impairment of precision movements, causing poor coordination. The incidence and duration of these reactions is unknown; side effects do not always resolve promptly on discontinuation of mefloquine. Estimated incidence of severe adverse effects, including epilepsy and psychosis, is 1 in 10 000. About 40% of side effects occur after the first two doses and 70% after three doses
Long-term use	Currently licensed in the UK for prophylaxis lasting 3 months but can safely be given for up to 1 year

Advice for travellers

Travellers should be warned about the adverse reactions which may occur in association with mefloquine

Stop taking mefloquine if experiencing symptoms such as dizziness, fits or unusual changes in mood such as depression, anxiety or confusion; alternative antimalarials should then be taken

Take second-choice antimalarials if very concerned about possible side effects; however, these offer less protection

DOXYCYCLINE *(unlicensed indication; take specialist advice before prescribing)*

Use	Useful for short- to medium-term prophylaxis in areas of multiple drug resistance; also used for adults with epilepsy who are visiting areas with chloroquine resistance
Adult dosage	100 mg daily
Length of prophylaxis	Start 1 week before travel and continue until 4 full weeks after leaving the malarious area
Children	Not recommended for children aged less than 12 years
Pregnancy	Not recommended
Breast-feeding	Not recommended
Contraindications	Pregnancy, breast-feeding, porphyria, systemic lupus erythematosus
Side effects	Can cause photosensitivity (cover up and use sun blocks) and oesophagitis (take after meals and with plenty of water)
Long-term use	Can be used for up to 3 months; effect of longer-term use is unknown

3.3 Special cases and malaria

Specialist advice should be sought when in doubt about the following groups and others with long-standing medical problems.

Former immigrants and their families: those who are visiting family and friends in malarious areas are at particularly high risk. Their partial immunity to malaria is lost relatively soon (several months) after leaving areas where malaria occurs and they do not seek advice or realise the need for prophylaxis. Also, in some areas, such as India, malaria transmission has increased since they emigrated. The usual recommended prophylaxis should be taken, along with preventive measures to avoid mosquito bites. Specialist advice should be sought if they are returning to live in malarious areas

Pregnant and breast-feeding women: *see Pregnant women*

Children: *see Children*

People without a spleen: such travellers are at increased risk of developing severe malaria. Ideally travel to malarious area should be avoided. Extra care should be taken with prophylaxis and anti-mosquito measures

Long-term travellers: expatriates who are living in malaria-endemic areas should continue prophylaxis for the duration of their stay because they will probably never develop protective immunity *(see Malaria prevention — prophylaxis).* Anti-mosquito measures are essential; the prophylaxis being used may be less than optimal *(see Malaria prevention — avoiding bites)*; advice about rapid diagnosis and treatment of malaria attacks should be given

Epileptic travellers: travellers with epilepsy should avoid taking chloroquine or mefloquine because both are epileptogenic. Proguanil can be used instead of chloroquine alone in areas where no chloroquine resistance occurs. For travel to areas where chloroquine resistance is present, doxycycline can be used for 3 months. Anticonvulsants may shorten the half-life of doxycycline but an increased dose is not recommended at present

Pilots and others who undertake precision activities: pilots should not take mefloquine because of the risk of side effects, including dizziness and impairment of precision movements. Chloroquine plus proguanil is the best option if travel includes areas where chloroquine-resistant malaria is present

Patients with renal failure: travellers with renal failure can take antimalarial drugs; however, the dose of chloroquine and proguanil may need to be reduced. In areas with a high risk of chloroquine-resistant malaria, mefloquine or doxycycline may be used because they are largely metabolized and excreted through the liver

3.4 Standby treatment

Standby treatment may be useful for travellers who are going to areas where malaria is present and who will be remote from health-care facilities. The drugs of choice for treatment depend on the resistance to prophylaxis in the areas to be visited.

Degree of drug resistance	Standby treatment
No chloroquine resistance	If the risk of contracting malaria is low, the traveller may not need prophylaxis. Chloroquine can then be used for standby treatment. If chloroquine is being taken for prophylaxis, use pyrimethamine–sulfadoxine for treatment
Some resistance, where chloroquine and proguanil are first-choice prophylaxis	Pyrimethamine–sulfadoxine or mefloquine or quinine
Areas with multidrug resistance, where mefloquine is first-choice prophylaxis	Quinine with tetracycline or with pyrimethamine–sulfadoxine
Areas with very high drug resistance, where doxycycline is first-choice prophylaxis	Quinine with tetracycline

Adult drug dosages for standby treatment

Drug	Dosage
Chloroquine	600 mg base on days 1 and 2, 300 mg on day 3
Pyrimethamine–sulfadoxine	75 mg pyrimethamine–1500 mg sulfadoxine Pyrimethamine–sulfadoxine should not be taken by people with a history of allergy to sulpha drugs
Quinine* plus pyrimethamine–sulfadoxine	600 mg quinine 3 times daily for 3 days, followed by 75 mg pyrimethamine–1500 mg sulfadoxine
Quinine* plus tetracycline	600 mg quinine 3 times daily for 3 days plus 250 mg tetracycline 4 times daily for 7 days
Mefloquine	500 mg twice with a 6 h interval (15 mg/kg) — significant risk of neuropsychiatric side effects

*Quinine should be given for 7 days in the treatment of malaria, but side effects may not be tolerated for this length of time; thus a 3-day course is suggested for standby treatment

We do not recommend the use of halofantrine as a standby drug. Halofantrine prolongs the QT interval and can cause arrhythmias in susceptible individuals; fatalities have occurred.

Advice for travellers

Instructions with standby treatment:

Carry a thermometer and clear written instructions: symptoms of malaria include a measurable fever (38.5°C or more) or influenza-like illness that develops more than 7 days after arrival in a malarious area

Find out how to take the standby treatment course, including timing and doses

Seek medical advice as soon as possible and have a blood test for malaria

Resume antimalarials 7 days after the first treatment dose unless malaria treatment is still being taken, when antimalarials should be resumed after the end of treatment

4 SPECIAL CASES AND TRAVEL

4.1 Pregnant women

Advice for travellers

Avoid unnecessary travel to areas where medical services may be poor and to malarious areas

Have adequate health insurance cover: many policies exclude pregnancy

Avoid travelling late in pregnancy: many airlines do not carry women beyond the 35th week of pregnancy (*see Flying*) and shipping lines are hesitant after the 36th week

If travel to a malarious area cannot be avoided, take the recommended precautions: antimalarials and bite avoidance (*see Special cases and malaria*)

Balance risk of vaccination against risk of disease

Avoid dehydration: this can result from heat, long journeys and diarrhoea

Avoid diarrhoea: antidiarrhoeal medicines should not be taken except when advised by a doctor (*see Diarrhoea*)

Vaccination

Ideally, any necessary vaccines should be given before pregnancy. Vaccination during pregnancy must be discussed with a doctor because the safety of many vaccines in pregnancy is not known. Pregnant women can still get diseases if they are not immune, so the risk of disease must be balanced against the risk of vaccination.

Vaccines that can be given: tetanus vaccine, inactivated polio vaccine and short-term protection against hepatitis A (human normal immunoglobulin); hepatitis A protection is advisable if travelling to a higher-risk area

Vaccines to be avoided unless risk of acquiring disease is great and travel is unavoidable: hepatitis A, inactivated polysaccharide typhoid, meningococcal A&C and rabies vaccines (the safety of these vaccines in pregnancy is unknown)

Vaccines to be avoided: live vaccines, namely oral polio, yellow fever, oral typhoid, BCG and MMR. If yellow fever vaccine is advised for a country, travelling to that country should be avoided while pregnant; if a yellow fever vaccination certificate is required only for entry purposes, a letter of exemption can be given

Oral polio and yellow fever vaccines have been given in pregnancy (inadvertently or during epidemics) without causing fetal damage. If the risk of disease is great, vaccination may be considered; a specialist should be consulted

Malaria

Pregnant women are more likely to develop life-threatening malaria, and spontaneous abortion and premature delivery can be induced. Unnecessary travel to malarious areas should be avoided. Extra care should be taken to avoid catching malaria, using all possible means. Medical attention must be sought promptly if any symptoms of malaria develop.

Prophylaxis

Chloroquine and proguanil are relatively safe during pregnancy. Folic acid supplements (5 mg daily or on alternate days) should be taken with proguanil. Although drugs are generally better avoided in pregnancy, pregnant women who must travel to malarious areas must take prophylaxis. The risk of severe illness or death from malaria is much greater than the risk of problems due to chloroquine or proguanil.

Mefloquine should be avoided during pregnancy, though it may be relatively safe in the second and third trimester. Advice about contraception should be given and conception avoided for 3 months after completion of mefloquine course.

Doxycycline should not be taken in pregnancy.

Breast-feeding women can take chloroquine and proguanil. Mefloquine and doxycycline should be avoided.

See Malaria prevention — prophylaxis.

4.2 Children

Advice for travellers

Avoid diarrhoea: oral rehydration fluids should be given during episodes of diarrhoea; antidiarrhoeal medication should not be used (*see Diarrhoea*)

Protect children from the sun: prickly heat and nappy rash are more common in hot climates (*see Sun*)

Ensure that children wear shoes: infections such as the dog hookworm gain entry through the skin *(see Insects, worms and other animals and Other common illnesses)*

Seek medical advice promptly if a feverish illness occurs; fever in a child is usually due to the same conditions that occur in this country, such as ear or throat infections, but malaria must be considered in areas where it is present, and other infections, such as meningitis and typhoid, are more common in some countries

Avoid travel sickness: this can affect children badly; they should avoid reading and other activities that are likely to worsen the condition while travelling; promethazine can be used to reduce nausea

Useful items to take include:

Disposable nappies and baby food

Analgesics or antipyretics, e.g. paracetamol, and oral rehydration salts *(see First-aid kits)*

Sufficient medication for any child currently taking medicine

Vaccination

Routine childhood vaccines: children should be up-to-date with diphtheria, pertussis, tetanus, polio, Hib (*haemophilus influenzae* type b), MMR and the appropriate boosters

Hepatitis A vaccine: hepatitis A is usually a very mild illness in children so protection for this age group is not a priority; however, there is a risk of transmitting the infection to adults on return (*see Vaccine guidelines [Appendix II]*)

Yellow fever vaccine: can safely be given to children aged more than 9 months; with younger babies, travel to high-risk areas should be avoided (*see Vaccine guidelines [Appendix II]*)

Typhoid vaccine: polysaccharide typhoid vaccine can be given to children aged more than 18 months; care with food, water and personal hygiene is important for prevention

Other vaccines: if children will be spending long periods in developing countries or will be staying in local conditions or attending local schools, other vaccines should be considered, such as BCG and hepatitis B, which can be given from birth; the lower age limit for most other vaccines is 12–18 months

See Vaccine guidelines (Appendix II).

Malaria

Babies and young children are particularly susceptible and can die rapidly from malaria.

Advice for travellers

Avoid unnecessary travel with babies and young children to areas where malaria is present, especially where the malaria is known to be resistant to the frequently prescribed drugs; no antimalarial is 100% effective

Avoid mosquito bites: DEET should be used only on the clothing of children aged less than 5 years, not directly on the skin; Mosiguard Natural containing derivatives of eucalyptus oil appears to be safe for children; mosquito cot nets are available

Take the appropriate antimalarial for the destination

Seek medical advice promptly if a feverish illness occurs

Medication must be kept out of reach of children: overdose can be fatal

Doses of prophylactic drugs for children

CHLOROQUINE*
PLUS PROGUANIL

Age	Weight (kg)	Fraction of adult dose
0–5 weeks	NA	0.125
6 weeks to 11 months	†	0.25
1–5 years	10–19	0.5
6–11 years	20–39	0.75
≥ 12 years	> 40	1

*Chloroquine is available as a syrup, but tablets can be broken and crushed. The required amount can be crushed into a small amount of water and followed by something to eat or drink to take away the bitter taste. †For infants and children aged more than 6 months, weight is a good guide for dose; chloroquine 5 mg/kg per week, proguanil 3 mg/kg per day. NA, not applicable.

MEFLOQUINE*

Age	Weight (kg)	Fraction of adult dose
2–5 years	15–19	0.25
6–8 years	20–30	0.5
9–11 years	31–45	0.75
≥ 12 years	> 45	1

*Not recommended for children weighing less than 15 kg

4.3 Former immigrants and visitors from developing countries

Former immigrants and their families who return to visit relatives and friends have the highest risk of any single category of traveller for contracting hepatitis A, typhoid fever and malaria while abroad. Various factors contribute to this:

- Belief that they have immunity
- Lack of awareness that protection is available
- Higher probability of travelling to rural areas, spending long periods abroad and staying under local conditions
- Less control over diet while away
- Unfamiliarity with health services in the UK

The general-practice surgery is in an excellent situation to address these problems. Practice nurses, general practitioners and other staff can use routine consultations to give opportunistic advice about the risk and prevention of malaria and other health problems likely to be encountered during visits to their homeland and to update routine vaccines.

See Special cases and malaria.

Hepatitis A

Hepatitis A immunity (due to infection in childhood) is often present in people who grew up in a developing country. A history of jaundice is rare in this situation because the infection is often subclinical in children. The hepatitis A antibody status of such people should be checked. If antibodies are present, immunity is usually lifelong. If no hepatitis A antibodies are present, protection is required.

See Vaccine guidelines (Appendix II).

4.4 Travellers with pre-existing health problems

Advice for travellers

Carry an adequate supply of usual medication (and an easily available record of this) and an emergency medical kit

Check for exclusions in health insurance

Contact the airline early if problems during flight are anticipated; they may be able to help or give advice (*see Flying*). Special facilities, such as oxygen, can often be provided if the airline is contacted in advance

A medical certificate of fitness for air travel may need to be completed by the patient's doctor

See Vaccine guidelines (Appendix II) and Malaria prevention — prophylaxis.

Heart disease

Recent myocardial infarction and uncontrolled cardiac failure are contraindications to flying. Symptoms may worsen if travel is stressful, and extra care should be taken while acclimatizing to a hot climate. Generally, symptoms should be no worse than while at home.

Respiratory disease

Patients with severe symptoms, such as those with chronic obstructive airways disease (COAD), are likely to have problems during flight and the airline must be contacted before travel. Respiratory infections are common throughout the world.

Gastrointestinal problems

Achlorhydria caused by gastrectomy or the use of H_2-receptor antagonists increases the risk of gut infections such as salmonellosis. Patients with Crohn's disease and ulcerative colitis should take special care with food and water while abroad, and travel to high-risk countries should be avoided because some gut infections can worsen symptoms and also may provoke a relapse of disease.

Current medication should be checked because immunosuppressive drugs may contraindicate the use of live vaccines.

Diabetes mellitus

Insulin must be carried in hand luggage. Schedules to allow for crossing time zones should be worked out in advance. Check with diabetic associations for more information on travel with diabetes and on medical insurance *(see British Diabetic Association [Appendix V])*.

HIV infection

See HIV-positive travellers and vaccination.

Health insurance and clearly labelled medication sufficient for the whole trip should be carried. Immunosuppressed patients are more susceptible to many infections but little is currently known about the risk of illness abroad.
Some countries require evidence of a negative HIV test as an entry requirement for certain categories of visitor. Consult the approved sources for the latest information *(see the Foreign Office and TRAVAX [Appendix IV])* but arrangements change. Checking with the embassy of the country concerned is advisable.

5 STAYING HEALTHY ABROAD

5.1 First-aid kits

Advice for travellers

Take a general first-aid kit containing:

Sterile plasters and gauze

Antiseptic cream

Analgesics and antipyretics, e.g. paracetamol

Oral rehydration sachets or tablets

After-sun and calamine lotion

Any usual medication taken

Sun cream (at least factor 15) and insect repellents

Consider carrying an emergency medical kit *(see below)*

Travellers who will be remote from medical care

Additional items must be considered depending on length and type of travel, age group and medical knowledge:

Antibiotics: a good combination is co-amoxiclav, ciprofloxacin and metronidazole; co-amoxiclav for various infections including urine and skin infections; ciprofloxacin for bacterial dysentery and severe travellers' diarrhoea; metronidazole for suspected amoebiasis or giardiasis

Antimalarial tablets for prophylaxis and standby treatment with instructions (*see Standby treatment*)

A moderately strong analgesic

Antihistamine tablets

Antidiarrhoeal agent such as loperamide (for adults only)

Chloramphenicol eye ointment

Anti-motion sickness medication

Antifungal cream

Giving sets and replacement fluids, if suitable expertise is available

A handbook is useful for advice on when and how to take medicines (*see Stay Healthy Abroad* and *Traveller's Health [Appendix V]*).

Many developing countries re-use medical supplies such as syringes and needles, increasing the risk of HIV and hepatitis B infection. To ensure personal safety, travellers can carry a kit containing syringes, needles and dressings in a properly labelled package, available from travel clinics, some chemists and camping shops. All medications and the emergency medical kit must be properly packaged and labelled. A small supply of medicines for personal use (preferably with the prescription) can usually be carried. If these guidelines are followed, customs difficulties are unlikely.

WHILE AWAY

5.2 Diarrhoea

Many infections, including travellers' diarrhoea, hepatitis A, typhoid, cholera and polio, are acquired by ingestion of contaminated food or water.

Travellers' diarrhoea is very common, about one-third of travellers to developing countries being affected during a 2-week stay. Most episodes are self-limiting and last 24 h or less. Symptoms usually include acute diarrhoea with abdominal cramps that may last a few days. The most common causative pathogen is enterotoxigenic *Escherichia coli*, followed by *Campylobacter, Salmonella* and *Giardia*.

Travellers' diarrhoea is particularly prevalent in developing countries and the New Independent States of the former USSR.

Advice for travellers

Prevention

Cook it, peel it or leave it: eat freshly cooked hot food; wash and peel fruit and vegetables (or cook them)

Drink only bottled (aerated if possible) or sterilized water (*see below*)

Avoid ice in drinks

Clean teeth with bottled water

Do not drink from lakes or rivers

Bottled and canned drinks are generally safe

Avoid reheated food, food that has been left standing or is exposed to flies; also, avoid shellfish, salad, ice-cream, mayonnaise (and other dishes containing uncooked egg) and unpasteurized milk, all of which carry a higher risk of causing diarrhoea

Ensure good personal hygiene

Treatment

Rehydration: drink plenty and continue to eat (adults)

In children, who dehydrate rapidly and may be more severely affected, give oral rehydration drinks in addition to other fluids and food

If a baby is being breast-fed, continue breast-feeding and offer rehydration fluids between feeds

If ready-made rehydration salts are not available, make a rehydration solution by adding 8 level teaspoons sugar and 1 level teaspoon salt to 1 litre clean water; the solution should taste only slightly salty; fruit juice can be added to improve the taste

Continued

Advice for travellers *continued*

Medication

Take loperamide in situations in which diarrhoea must be stopped, such as during long journeys; it should not be given to children

If remote from medical care, consider taking some antibiotics, such as ciprofloxacin, which may shorten the length of illness; however, side effects can occur and regular use of these antibiotics encourages the development of resistance, subsequently limiting their use in the treatment of severe illness. Antibiotic use is better reserved for dysentery or persistent diarrhoea

Medical help should be sought in the following circumstances:

Blood in the stool

Fever (though a transitory fever sometimes occurs with travellers' diarrhoea)

Diarrhoea for more than 3 days

Drowsiness or confusion

Children with frequent diarrhoea or blood in the stool or who remain unwell, have other symptoms such as fever, vomiting, drowsiness, or are passing little urine

Water sterilization

Advice for travellers

Water to be sterilized must be taken from a reasonable source, such as tap water

Boiling: the most effective method; water must be brought to the boil; at high altitudes it must be boiled for several minutes

Filtration: does not remove all germs when used alone; to obtain the best result, it should be used with disinfection; several small, easy-to-carry filters are available; some include disinfection

Disinfection: less effective than the previous two methods; tincture of iodine should be used in preference to chlorine, unless used long term
Tincture of iodine: use 4 drops of a 2% solution to 1 litre of water; leave to stand for 30 min; do not use for more than a few weeks
Chlorine: tablet form, follow instructions; bleach, 1–2 drops of 5% solution in 1 litre of water

5.3 Sexually transmitted disease and contraception

Anyone who has casual sex risks catching a sexually transmitted disease, such as HIV, hepatitis B, gonorrhoea, syphilis and chlamydia.

Sexually transmitted diseases and HIV

In many countries, HIV is much more common than in the UK *(see map)*, including countries within Europe. In some areas, up to 90% of prostitutes and 30% of the local population are infected. Recent figures show that 79% of heterosexually acquired HIV infections in England and Wales have been acquired abroad [*Communicable Disease Report* 1996, **6**:R1].

Estimated distribution of HIV-infected adults, mid-1995

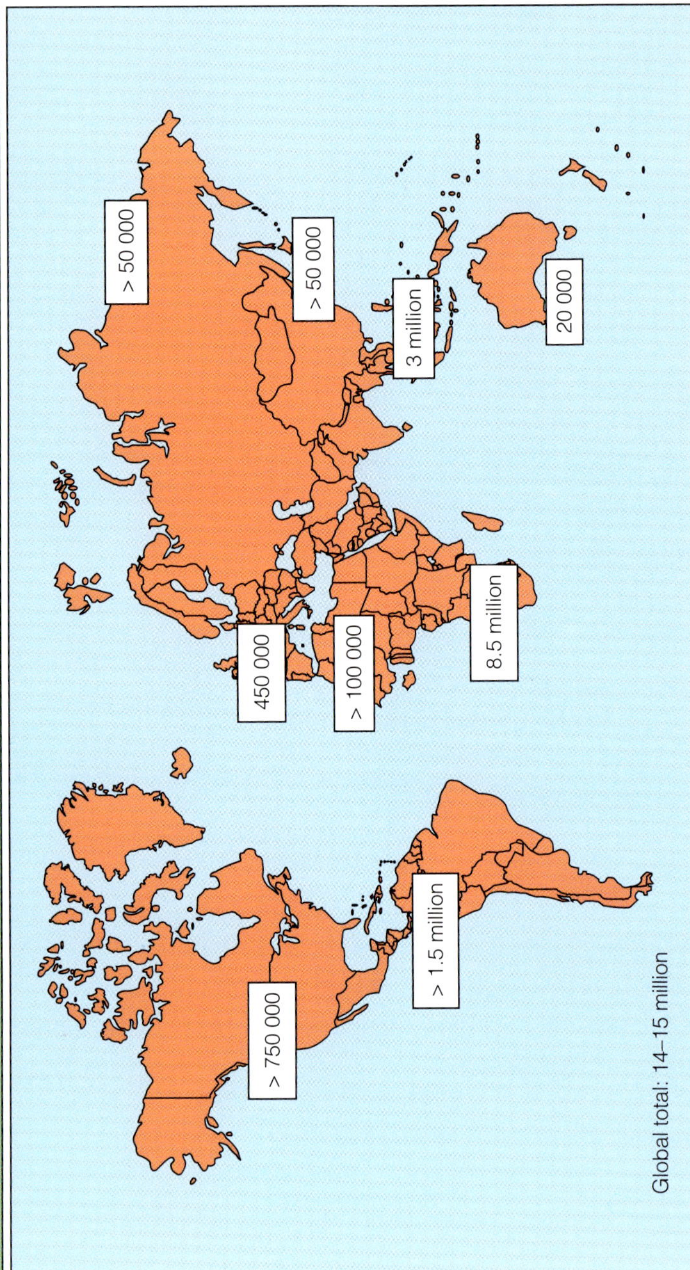

The misconception that HIV is a disease confined to homosexuals and drug abusers is still prevalent. Worldwide, HIV is most often caught from sex between a man and a woman. Travellers should be made aware of this, advised to use condoms if they put themselves at risk, and reminded that people with HIV infection do not usually look ill.

Advice for travellers

If you have sex, make it safer by using a condom: these provide good but not complete protection

Buy condoms before you travel: look for the British Standards kitemark

Avoid unnecessary medical or dental treatment, and blood transfusions unless essential

Do not have a tattoo, acupuncture or body piercing

Remember alcohol weakens inhibitions and can cause precautions to be forgotten

Transmission of HIV can occur through the re-use of medical supplies; commercially prepared travel kits are available (*see First-aid kits*).

Some organizations will courier screened blood to members if a transfusion is required (*see The Blood Care Foundation [Appendix V]).*

The oral contraceptive pill

- All travel vaccinations can be given
- The oral contraceptive pill does not interact with chloroquine, proguanil and mefloquine. If doxycycline is recommended, additional contraceptive precautions should be used during the first 2 weeks of prophylaxis
- If diarrhoea and vomiting occur or antibiotics are taken, another method of contraception should be used in addition to the pill during the illness, while on antibiotics and for 7 days afterwards
- If a pill is missed or is taken late, another method of contraception should be used for the next 7 days
- Crossing time zones can cause confusion. Some women find it simpler to stick to 'home time' wherever they are, although this can be difficult if it involves taking a pill in the middle of the night. Another option is to take it at the same time of day, for example at bedtime. Care should be taken that no more than 27 h elapse from one pill to the next. Taking two pills on the same day may be necessary during the change over (one at the 'old' time and one at the 'new' time); the second pill should be taken from a spare pack of pills so that the usual sequence is not disturbed

5.4 Accidents

Swimming and traffic accidents are among the leading causes of death in travellers. Many accidents are avoidable. The influence of alcohol should always be remembered.

Extra caution should be taken with dangerous sports while abroad; equipment and safety procedures are inadequate in many countries. Such activities are not usually covered by standard travel insurance.

Advice for travellers

Driving

Avoid using motorcycles and mopeds

Use available safety equipment

Avoid travel at night

Select a safe car: check for seat belts, good tyres and brakes

Rent a large vehicle when possible

Find out about local road signs and traffic laws

Carry a first-aid kit

Swimming

Carefully select safe swimming areas: check for strong currents and undertows, jelly fish, sharks, hippopotami

Avoid bathing in fresh-water lakes and rivers in tropical and subtropical areas: the infection schistosomiasis (bilharzia) is often present *(see Insects, worms and animals*)

Avoid bathing in polluted water

Use protective footwear, especially where sea urchins or coral are present

5.5 Sun

Sunburn can cause much discomfort. Excessive sun exposure leads to premature skin ageing. Increasing evidence suggests that excessive sun exposure, particularly sunburn when aged less than 15 years, is a major risk factor for skin cancer in later life.

Advice for travellers

Prevention

Cover up and wear a sun hat; use high-factor sun creams (factor 15 or higher)

Avoid the midday sun (11.00 to 15.00)

Take special care with babies and children and with pale skin

Drink plenty of non-alcoholic fluids

Remember that people often get sunburnt while swimming

Continued

Advice for travellers *continued*

Treatment

In case of sunburn, drink plenty, use calamine lotion and moisturizing lotions

If the burn is severe, seek medical attention

In case of prickly heat, an irritating itchy rash that occurs often in hot humid climates, reduce sweating by wearing loose cotton clothing, frequent bathing in cool water and application of talcum powder. Use calamine lotion and oral antihistamines to relieve the itchiness

In case of heat exhaustion, causing nausea, vomiting, headache, lethargy and dizziness, rehydration with oral rehydration drinks and rest is advised

In case of heat stroke, rare but a medical emergency when it occurs, with symptoms including a temperature of 40°C or more, no sweating and rapid loss of consciousness, seek medical help immediately; the patient must be cooled and rehydrated under medical supervision

5.6 Insects, worms and other animals

Mosquitoes

Mosquitoes carry many infections, including malaria, dengue fever, and Japanese encephalitis *(see Vaccine guidelines [Appendix II] and Malaria and the traveller).*

Dengue fever is a viral infection common in many parts of Asia, the Caribbean and Central and South America; it is also present in Africa. Transmission is by mosquitoes, which bite during the day and at night. It causes an influenza-like illness, with fever, headache, and a rash, lasting for about 1 week. No specific cure exists but most people recover with no treatment. No vaccine is available, and prevention is achieved by avoiding mosquito bites (*see Malaria prevention — avoiding bites).*

Other insects

Some other insects can transmit infections to people, including sleeping sickness transmitted by tsetse flies and leishmaniasis by sandflies. However, such infections occur rarely in tourists spending only a few weeks abroad. More often tourists are troubled by the local reaction to the bite, usually redness, slight swelling and itchiness.

Advice for travellers

Do not scratch bites: it increases the risk of infection

Apply bland soothing creams

Take antihistamine tablets for more severe reactions

Seek medical advice if much swelling, fever, or severe allergy symptoms occur

Other hazards

Schistosomiasis (bilharzia): schistosomiasis is present in freshwater lakes and rivers in many areas of Africa and the Middle East and some parts of South America and the Far East. The parasite penetrates the skin and can cause acute and chronic symptoms *(see Illness in the returned traveller)*

Worm infections: certain worms, present in sand and soil in many tropical and subtropical areas, can infect people through the skin

Rabies: this fatal infection is transmitted by the bites (sometimes licks or scratches) of infected animals

Scorpion stings and spider bites: scorpion stings are usually extremely painful; some can cause internal damage and medical help should be sought. Only a few spiders can inject venom into people: if bitten, medical help should be sought

Snake bites: snakes do not attack people without provocation. Serious poisoning and death rarely occur, particularly if adequate medical help is received within a few hours of the bite
Antivenom should only be used by a doctor or a medical assistant who is experienced in antivenom administration

Advice for travellers

Avoid swimming or paddling in lakes and rivers in Africa *(see Accidents)*

Wear footwear and avoid lying directly on the sand, especially when above the high-water line

Do not stroke cats and dogs; avoid contact with wild animals

If bitten or licked by a possibly rabid animal: clean the wound with soap or detergent and running water for 5 min; apply an antiseptic such as iodine or 40–70% alcohol; seek medical help immediately

Consider pre-exposure rabies vaccination if travelling to remote areas *(see Vaccine guidelines [Appendix II])*

Check shoes and clothing for scorpions and spiders before putting them on; if bitten seek medical help

Wear boots and use a torch at night to avoid stepping on a snake by accident

In case of a snake bite: do not incise; wipe the site of the bite; apply a broad, firm (but not tight) bandage to cover the bitten limb; move the limb as little as possible; seek medical help immediately

5.7 Flying

Contraindications to travel in pressurized aircraft on scheduled flights include:

- Severe otitis media and sinusitis
- Acute contagious or communicable disease
- Contagious severe skin disease
- Severe anaemia

- Mental illness without escort or sedation
- Recent myocardial infarction
- Uncontrolled cardiac failure
- Recent cerebral infarction
- Peptic ulceration with haemorrhage within 3 weeks
- Simple abdominal operation within 10 days
- Major chest surgery within 14 days
- Wired fractures of the mandible
- Introduction of air into body cavities within 7 days
- Pregnancy after 35th week for international journeys, 36th week for short journeys
- Scuba diving within 12 h of flight

Advice for travellers

Contact the airline early if problems during flight are anticipated; they may be able to give advice or provide special facilities

Avoid dehydration, which can lead to extra fatigue and headaches: drink plenty of water or unsweetened soft drinks during the flight and limit alcohol and caffeine consumption; a particular problem on long-haul flights

Stretch regularly and walk about to reduce ankle swelling and lessen stiffness during the flight

Try to sleep for a while during long flights

Avoid caffeinated drinks before and during the flight if anxious; mild sedation taken on the day before and the day of travel can be used for those who are extremely anxious

Try yawning, swallowing or similar manoeuvres to help to clear the eustachian tubes, especially in case of a bad cold or ear infection, which may cause severe pain during ascent or descent; nasal decongestants are sometimes helpful

To lessen jet lag, limit alcohol and caffeine during the flight and try to arrive 24 h before important business meetings or other similar commitments; a short-acting benzodiazepine is sometimes useful for the first 1–3 nights after the flight for business travellers on short trips who have experienced a time change of several hours or more

6 THE RETURNED TRAVELLER

6.1 Malaria prevention: continuing prophylaxis

Prophylaxis should be continued for 4 full weeks after leaving a malarious area. If problematic side effects occur during this period, causing the original prophylaxis to be discontinued, the course should be completed with the second-choice prophylaxis for the area visited. Alternatively, prophylaxis can be stopped; any fever or influenza-like illness must be investigated promptly.

6.2 Illness in the returned traveller

A few important or common diagnoses are mentioned briefly here. For more information seek suitable expert advice or refer to the literature *(see Further study [Appendix III])*. Many other infections, such as leprosy, tuberculosis, leishmaniasis and onchocerciasis, may need to be considered, especially in former immigrants and those who have lived and worked in developing countries.

Fever

Fever may be caused by malaria. Other imported infections to consider are dengue fever *(see Insects, worms and other animals — mosquitoes)*, hepatitis, pneumonia (remember legionnaire's disease), acute schistosomiasis (Katayama fever), typhoid, tick typhus and HIV seroconversion illness. If the diagnosis is unclear in a sick patient, a specialist in tropical or infectious diseases should be consulted.

Malaria

Malaria must be considered in anyone who has visited a malarious area. Fever can be intermittent, and other common symptoms include headache, generalized aching, shivering, vomiting, and diarrhoea. Only one or two of these may be present. Malaria can occur several years after exposure, although falciparum malaria usually manifests within 3 months.

Malaria can only be diagnosed by examination of a blood film. Thick and thin blood films should be examined immediately, on the day of presentation in a patient with suspicious symptoms. More than one film may need to be examined. If malaria is diagnosed or if the diagnosis is in doubt, expert advice should be sought.

Diarrhoea

Travellers' diarrhoea may occur shortly after return. Most patients need symptomatic treatment only.

Examination of fresh stool samples and appropriate treatment are required in some cases, for example when fever is present (consider bacillary dysentery and malaria), when blood is present in the stools (in an acute infection, consider bacillary or amoebic dysentery), if diarrhoea becomes chronic (often resulting from giardia and amoebic infections).

Schistosomiasis (bilharzia)

This helminth infection is seen with increasing frequency in returning travellers, particularly from Africa. A few weeks after initial infection, an acute illness (Katayama fever) sometimes occurs, characterized by fever and generalized aches; urticaria may be present. Eosinophilia is usually marked but schistosome eggs are often absent from the urine and stool at this stage and serology is usually negative. More chronically, the individual may develop bloody diarrhoea or haematuria. A specialist should always be consulted for diagnosis and treatment.

Cutaneous larva migrans

Caused by the larva of a dog hookworm, this serpentine-shaped, itchy, often blistering, red track is regularly seen in travellers returning from tropical areas, especially the Caribbean, where the larva is often present in the sand and soil. Single tracks can be treated with 10% thiabendazole ointment, applied to the track, then occluded, once daily for 5 days.

6.3 Screening the asymptomatic returned traveller

A check-up is advisable for travellers who have been at particular risk of contracting a tropical disease. These include:

- People living or working under local conditions
- Those who have spent long periods abroad (6 months or more)
- Those who have had definite exposure to infections, such as schistosomiasis, onchocerciasis, filariasis and HIV
- Those who have had a severe infection abroad, such as malaria or severe diarrhoea with blood

Travellers may request screening because of specific concerns such as HIV infection and the risk of passing on infections to close contacts.

When to screen

Ideally screening in asymptomatic people should take place at least 3 months after return because some infections, such as schistosomiasis, are difficult to exclude before this time. Screening for HIV infection should be done at least 3 months after exposure and may need to be repeated.

Useful screening tests

- Stool examination for cysts, ova and parasites
- Urine analysis
- Full blood count and differential count (eosinophilia may be due to parasitosis)
- Specific tests such as HIV, schistosomiasis or filaria serology if appropriate

Some tests may need to be performed at a specialist laboratory where staff have a greater familiarity with unusual parasites.

APPENDIX I: COUNTRY GUIDELINES

The recommendations given have been agreed by doctors at the Liverpool School of Tropical Medicine. They may differ from advice given elsewhere. We do not usually recommend typhoid vaccination for many tourists or business travellers whose trip will last only a few weeks *(see Vaccine guidelines [Appendix II]).*

The guidelines are presented in two sections:

- **Vaccinations** advised for all travellers, including those on package tours and additional vaccines for those who will be living under local conditions or living abroad (Ls/local).
  Routine childhood vaccines: all children should be up-to-date with these
  Diphtheria vaccine for travellers to the New Independent States of the former USSR: all travellers to these countries should have received a primary course of diphtheria vaccine. A booster dose is recommended (if last dose was more than 10 years ago) for those who are going to live or work with local people

  BCG vaccine: recommendations for travellers are given in the individual vaccine guidelines

  Tick-borne encephalitis vaccine: occasionally recommended for hiking and camping trips in some forested areas of Europe (*see Vaccine guidelines [Appendix II]*)

  Yellow fever vaccine: can be required or recommended *(see Vaccine guidelines [Appendix II])*; recommendations are given here

- **Risk of malaria** in the country (if applicable) according to the World Heath Organization and British guidelines. Recommendations for prophylaxis are given (second-choice regimen in parentheses); the most up-to-date recommendations should always be followed. Specialist advice should be sought in case of uncertainty about prophylaxis (e.g. complicated itineraries, contraindications).

  For advice about avoiding mosquito bites *see Malaria prevention — avoiding bites.*

  In some areas the risk of malaria is given as low or very low. Here, prophylaxis is unnecessary, but care should be taken to avoid bites; in the event of a fever or influenza-like illness, malaria should be considered.

  MEF, mefloquine; CHL, chloroquine; PRO, proguanil; DOX, doxycycline *(see Malaria prevention — prophylaxis)*

Countries excluded include a few non-malarious islands rarely visited by travellers and countries of western and southern Europe, Canada, the USA, Australia and New Zealand, where the vaccines usually recommended are the same as in the UK. Childhood vaccines should be up-to-date and adults should be up-to-date with tetanus vaccine.

A good atlas is useful when consulting these guidelines.

AFGHANISTAN

Vaccines: Hepatitis A, polio, tetanus, typhoid
Ls/local: Consider BCG, diphtheria, hepatitis B, Japanese encephalitis, rabies
Malaria: Below 2000 m; risk exists; May to November; some chloroquine resistance
Prophylaxis in risk areas: CHL + PRO (MEF)

ALBANIA

Vaccines: Hepatitis A, polio, tetanus
Ls/local: Typhoid; consider BCG, diphtheria, hepatitis B, rabies

ALGERIA

Vaccines: Hepatitis A, polio, tetanus
Ls/local: Typhoid; consider BCG, diphtheria, hepatitis B, rabies
Malaria: Small isolated focus in Ihrir only; limited risk; year round; no chloroquine resistance
No prophylaxis, avoid mosquito bites

AMERICAN SAMOA

Vaccines: Hepatitis A, polio, tetanus
Ls/local: Typhoid; consider BCG, diphtheria, hepatitis B

ANGOLA

Vaccines: Hepatitis A, polio, tetanus, yellow fever
Ls/local: Typhoid; consider BCG, diphtheria, hepatitis B, meningococcal A&C, rabies
Malaria: All areas; high risk; year round; chloroquine resistance reported
Prophylaxis: MEF (CHL + PRO)

ANTIGUA AND BARBUDA

Vaccines: Polio, tetanus
Ls/local: Hepatitis A, typhoid; consider BCG, diphtheria, hepatitis B

ARGENTINA

Vaccines: Hepatitis A, polio, tetanus
Ls/local: Typhoid; consider BCG, diphtheria, hepatitis B, rabies
Malaria: Rural areas below 1200 m along the borders with Bolivia and Paraguay; risk exists; October to May; no chloroquine resistance
Prophylaxis in risk areas: CHL (PRO)

ARMENIA

Vaccines: Diphtheria, hepatitis A, polio, tetanus
Ls/local: Typhoid; consider BCG, hepatitis B, rabies

AZERBAIJAN
Vaccines: Diphtheria, hepatitis A, polio, tetanus
Ls/local: Typhoid; consider BCG, hepatitis B, rabies
Malaria: Southern areas and Kachmas region in north; risk exists; year round; no chloroquine resistance
Prophylaxis: CHL (PRO)
All other areas, including Baku; no risk
No prophylaxis, avoid mosquito bites

BAHAMAS
Vaccines: Polio, tetanus
Ls/local: Hepatitis A, typhoid; consider diphtheria, hepatitis B

BAHRAIN
Vaccines: Hepatitis A, polio, tetanus
Ls/local: Typhoid; consider BCG, diphtheria, hepatitis B

BANGLADESH
Vaccines: Hepatitis A, polio, tetanus, typhoid
Ls/local: Consider BCG, diphtheria, hepatitis B, Japanese encephalitis, rabies
Malaria: Dhaka city; no risk
No prophylaxis, avoid mosquito bites
Chittagong Hill tracts (forested areas and south-east); risk exists; year round; high chloroquine resistance
Prophylaxis: MEF (CHL + PRO)
All other areas; risk exists; year round; moderate chloroquine resistance
Prophylaxis: CHL + PRO (MEF)

BARBADOS
Vaccines: Polio, tetanus
Ls/local: Hepatitis A, typhoid; consider diphtheria, hepatitis B

BELARUS
Vaccines: Diphtheria, hepatitis A, polio, tetanus
Ls/local: Typhoid; consider BCG, hepatitis B, rabies

BELIZE
Vaccines: Hepatitis A, polio, tetanus
Ls/local: Typhoid; consider BCG, diphtheria, hepatitis B, rabies
Malaria: Belize District and urban areas; low risk
No prophylaxis, avoid mosquito bites
All other areas; risk exists; year round; no chloroquine resistance
Prophylaxis: CHL (PRO)

BENIN
Vaccines: Hepatitis A, polio, tetanus, yellow fever
Ls/local: Typhoid; consider BCG, diphtheria, hepatitis B, meningococcal A&C, rabies
Malaria: All areas; high risk; year round; chloroquine resistance reported
Prophylaxis: MEF (CHL + PRO)

BERMUDA
Vaccines: Polio, tetanus
Ls/local: Hepatitis A, typhoid; consider diphtheria, hepatitis B

BHUTAN
Vaccines: Hepatitis A, polio, tetanus, typhoid
Ls/local: Consider BCG, diphtheria, hepatitis B, rabies
Malaria: Southern belt of Chirang, Gaylegphug, Samchi, Samdrupjongkhar and Shemgang; risk exists; year round; chloroquine resistance reported
Prophylaxis in risk areas: CHL + PRO (MEF)

BOLIVIA
Vaccines: Hepatitis A, polio, tetanus, yellow fever
Ls/local: Typhoid; consider BCG, diphtheria, hepatitis B, rabies
Malaria: Rural areas below 2500 m; risk exists; year round; chloroquine resistance reported
Prophylaxis: CHL + PRO (MEF)
Amazon basin region (borders with Brazil); risk exists; year round; high chloroquine resistance
Prophylaxis: MEF (CHL + PRO)
Urban areas and areas above 2500 m; little or no risk
No prophylaxis, avoid mosquito bites

BOSNIA AND HERZEGOVINA
Vaccines: Hepatitis A, polio, tetanus
Ls/local: Diphtheria, typhoid; consider BCG, hepatitis B, rabies

BOTSWANA
Vaccines: Hepatitis A, polio, tetanus
Ls/local: Typhoid; consider BCG, diphtheria, hepatitis B, rabies
Malaria: Northern half of country; high risk; November to June; chloroquine resistance reported
Prophylaxis in risk areas: CHL + PRO (MEF)

BRAZIL
Vaccines: Hepatitis A, polio, tetanus, yellow fever
Ls/local: Typhoid; consider BCG, diphtheria, hepatitis B, rabies
Malaria: Amazon basin region; risk exists; year round; high chloroquine resistance
Prophylaxis: MEF (CHL + PRO)
All other areas, including Rio de Janeiro and Sao Paulo; low risk
No prophylaxis, avoid mosquito bites

BRITISH VIRGIN ISLANDS
Vaccines: Polio, tetanus
Ls/local: Hepatitis A, typhoid; consider BCG, hepatitis B

BRUNEI DARUSSALAM
Vaccines: Hepatitis A, polio, tetanus
Ls/local: Typhoid; consider BCG, diphtheria, hepatitis B, Japanese encephalitis, rabies

BULGARIA
Vaccines: Hepatitis A, polio, tetanus
Ls/local: Diphtheria, typhoid; consider hepatitis B, rabies

BURKINA FASO
Vaccines: Hepatitis A, polio, tetanus, yellow fever
Ls/local: Typhoid; consider BCG, diphtheria, hepatitis A, meningococcal A&C, rabies
Malaria: All areas; high risk; year round; chloroquine resistance
Prophylaxis: MEF (CHL + PRO)

BURMA *see* MYANMAR

BURUNDI
Vaccines: Hepatitis A, polio, tetanus, yellow fever
Ls/local: Typhoid; consider BCG, diphtheria, hepatitis B, meningococcal A&C, rabies
Malaria: All areas; high risk; year round; chloroquine resistance
Prophylaxis: MEF (CHL + PRO)

CAMBODIA
Vaccines: Hepatitis A, polio, tetanus
Ls/local: Typhoid; consider BCG, diphtheria, hepatitis B, Japanese encephalitis, rabies
Malaria: Phnom Penh; low risk
No prophylaxis, avoid mosquito bites
Western border areas; risk exists; year round; mefloquine resistance reported
Prophylaxis: DOX (MEF)
All other areas; risk exists; year round; high chloroquine resistance
Prophylaxis: MEF (DOX)

CAMEROON
Vaccines: Hepatitis A, polio, tetanus, yellow fever
Ls/local: Typhoid; consider BCG, diphtheria, hepatitis B, meningococcal A&C, rabies
Malaria: All areas; high risk; year round; chloroquine resistance reported
Prophylaxis: MEF (CHL + PRO)

CAPE VERDE
Vaccines: Hepatitis A, polio, tetanus
Ls/local: Typhoid; consider BCG, diphtheria, hepatitis B, rabies
Malaria: Sao Tiago Island only; limited risk; September to November
No prophylaxis, avoid mosquito bites

CAYMAN ISLANDS
Vaccines: Hepatitis A, polio, tetanus
Ls/local: Typhoid; consider BCG, diphtheria, hepatitis B

CENTRAL AFRICAN REPUBLIC
Vaccines: Hepatitis A, polio, tetanus, yellow fever
Ls/local: Typhoid; consider BCG, diphtheria, hepatitis B, meningococcal A&C, rabies
Malaria: All areas; high risk; year round; chloroquine resistance reported
Prophylaxis: MEF (CHL + PRO)

CHAD
Vaccines: Hepatitis A, polio, tetanus, yellow fever
Ls/local: Typhoid; consider BCG, diphtheria, hepatitis B, meningococcal A&C, rabies
Malaria: All areas; high risk; year round; chloroquine resistance reported
Prophylaxis: MEF (CHL + PRO)

CHILE
Vaccines: Hepatitis A, polio, tetanus
Ls/local: Typhoid; consider BCG, diphtheria, hepatitis B, rabies

CHINA
Vaccines: Hepatitis A, polio, tetanus
Ls/local: Typhoid; consider BCG, diphtheria, hepatitis B, Japanese encephalitis, rabies
Malaria: Remote rural areas; risk exists; year round; no chloroquine resistance
Prophylaxis: CHL (PRO)
Hainan and Yunnan provinces; risk exists; year round; chloroquine resistance reported
Prophylaxis: MEF (CHL + PRO)
All other areas, including most tourist areas; very low risk
No prophylaxis, avoid mosquito bites

COLOMBIA
Vaccines: Hepatitis A, polio, tetanus, yellow fever
Ls/local: Typhoid; consider BCG, diphtheria, hepatitis B, rabies
Malaria: Rural areas below 800 m, including the Pacific coast and Amazon basin region; risk exists; year round; high chloroquine resistance
Prophylaxis: MEF (CHL + PRO)
All other areas, including Cartegena and Bogota; low risk
No prophylaxis, avoid mosquito bites

COMOROS

Vaccines: Hepatitis A, polio, tetanus
Ls/local: Typhoid; consider BCG, diphtheria, hepatitis B, rabies
Malaria: All areas; high risk; year round; chloroquine resistance reported
Prophylaxis: MEF (CHL + PRO)

CONGO

Vaccines: Hepatitis A, polio, tetanus, yellow fever
Ls/local: Typhoid; consider BCG, diphtheria, hepatitis B, meningococcal A&C, rabies
Malaria: All areas; high risk; year round; chloroquine resistance reported
Prophylaxis: MEF (CHL + PRO)

COOK ISLANDS

Vaccines: Hepatitis A, polio, tetanus
Ls/local: Typhoid; consider BCG, diphtheria, hepatitis B

COSTA RICA

Vaccines: Hepatitis A, polio, tetanus
Ls/local: Typhoid; consider BCG, diphtheria, hepatitis B, rabies
Malaria: Rural areas below 700 m; risk exists; year round; no chloroquine resistance
Prophylaxis in risk areas: CHL (PRO)

CROATIA

Vaccines: Hepatitis A, polio, tetanus
Ls/local: Diphtheria, typhoid; consider BCG, hepatitis B, rabies

CUBA

Vaccines: Hepatitis A, polio, tetanus
Ls/local: Typhoid; consider BCG, diphtheria, hepatitis B, rabies

CYPRUS

Vaccines: Tetanus, polio
Ls/local: Hepatitis A; consider hepatitis B, typhoid

CZECH REPUBLIC

Vaccines: Tetanus, polio, hepatitis A
Ls/local: Diphtheria, typhoid; consider hepatitis B, rabies

DJIBOUTI

Vaccines: Hepatitis A, polio, tetanus
Ls/local: Typhoid; consider BCG, diphtheria, hepatitis B, meningococcal A&C, rabies
Malaria: All areas; high risk; year round; chloroquine resistance reported
Prophylaxis: MEF (CHL + PRO)

DOMINICA

Vaccines: Hepatitis A, polio, tetanus
Ls/local: Typhoid; consider BCG, diphtheria, hepatitis B

DOMINICAN REPUBLIC
Vaccines: Hepatitis A, polio, tetanus
Ls/local: Typhoid; consider BCG, diphtheria, hepatitis B, rabies
Malaria: Most areas; risk exists; year round; no chloroquine resistance
Prophylaxis: CHL (PRO)

ECUADOR
Vaccines: Hepatitis A, polio, tetanus, yellow fever
Ls/local: Typhoid; consider BCG, diphtheria, hepatitis B, rabies
Malaria: Below 1500 m; risk exists; year round;
chloroquine resistance reported
Prophylaxis in risk areas: CHL + PRO (MEF)

EGYPT
Vaccines: Hepatitis A, polio, tetanus
Ls/local: Typhoid; consider BCG, diphtheria, hepatitis B, rabies
Malaria: El Faiyum area; risk exists; June to October;
no chloroquine resistance
Prophylaxis: CHL (PRO)
All other areas, including tourist areas; very low risk
No prophylaxis, avoid mosquito bites

EL SALVADOR
Vaccines: Hepatitis A, polio, tetanus
Ls/local: Typhoid; consider BCG, diphtheria, hepatitis B, rabies
Malaria: All areas, greatest below 600 m; risk exists; year round;
no chloroquine resistance
Prophylaxis: CHL (PRO)

EQUATORIAL GUINEA
Vaccines: Hepatitis A, polio, tetanus, yellow fever
Ls/local: Typhoid; consider BCG, diphtheria, hepatitis B, rabies
Malaria: All areas; high risk; year round; chloroquine resistance reported
Prophylaxis: MEF (CHL + PRO)

ERITREA
Vaccines: Hepatitis A, polio, tetanus
Ls/local: Typhoid; consider BCG, diphtheria, hepatitis B,
meningococcal A&C, rabies
Malaria: Below 2000 m; high risk; year round; chloroquine resistance
reported
Prophylaxis: MEF (CHL + PRO)
Above 2000 m, including Asmara; low or no risk
No prophylaxis, avoid mosquito bites

ESTONIA
Vaccines: Diphtheria, hepatitis A, polio, tetanus
Ls/local: Typhoid; consider BCG, hepatitis B, rabies

ETHIOPIA
Vaccines: Hepatitis A, polio, tetanus, yellow fever
Ls/local: Typhoid; consider BCG, diphtheria, hepatitis B, meningococcal A&C, rabies
Malaria: Below 2000 m; high risk; year round; chloroquine resistance reported
Prophylaxis: MEF (CHL + PRO)
Above 2000 m, including Addis Ababa; low or no risk
No prophylaxis, avoid mosquito bites

FALKLAND ISLANDS
Vaccines: Hepatitis A, polio, tetanus
Ls/local: Typhoid; consider diphtheria, hepatitis B, rabies

FIJI
Vaccines: Hepatitis A, polio, tetanus
Ls/local: Typhoid; consider BCG, diphtheria, hepatitis B

FRENCH GUIANA
Vaccines: Hepatitis A, polio, tetanus, yellow fever
Ls/local: Typhoid; consider BCG, diphtheria, hepatitis B, rabies
Malaria: All areas; risk exists; year round; chloroquine resistance reported
Prophylaxis: MEF (CHL + PRO)

FRENCH POLYNESIA
Vaccines: Hepatitis A, polio, tetanus
Ls/local: Typhoid; consider BCG, diphtheria, hepatitis B

GABON
Vaccines: Hepatitis A, polio, tetanus, yellow fever
Ls/local: Typhoid; consider BCG, diphtheria, hepatitis B, rabies
Malaria: All areas; high risk; year round; chloroquine resistance reported
Prophylaxis: MEF (CHL + PRO)

GAMBIA
Vaccines: Hepatitis A, polio, tetanus, yellow fever
Ls/local: Typhoid; consider BCG, diphtheria, hepatitis B, meningococcal A&C, rabies
Malaria: All areas; high risk; year round; chloroquine resistance reported
Prophylaxis: MEF (CHL + PRO)

GEORGIA
Vaccines: Diphtheria, hepatitis A, polio, tetanus
Ls/local: Typhoid; consider BCG, hepatitis B, rabies

GHANA
Vaccines: Hepatitis A, polio, tetanus, yellow fever
Ls/local: Typhoid; consider BCG, diphtheria, hepatitis B, meningococcal A&C, rabies
Malaria: All areas; high risk; year round; chloroquine resistance reported
Prophylaxis: MEF (CHL + PRO)

GRENADA
Vaccines: Hepatitis A, polio, tetanus
Ls/local: Typhoid; consider BCG, diphtheria, hepatitis B, rabies

GUADELOUPE
Vaccines: Hepatitis A, polio, tetanus
Ls/local: Typhoid; consider BCG, diphtheria, hepatitis B

GUAM
Vaccines: Hepatitis A, polio, tetanus
Ls/local: Typhoid; consider BCG, diphtheria, hepatitis B

GUATEMALA
Vaccines: Hepatitis A, polio, tetanus
Ls/local: Typhoid; consider BCG, diphtheria, hepatitis B, rabies
Malaria: Below 1500 m; risk exists; year round; no chloroquine resistance
Prophylaxis in risk areas: CHL (PRO)

GUINEA
Vaccines: Hepatitis A, polio, tetanus, yellow fever
Ls/local: Typhoid; consider BCG, diphtheria, hepatitis B, meningococcal A&C, rabies
Malaria: All areas; high risk; year round; chloroquine resistance reported
Prophylaxis: MEF (CHL + PRO)

GUINEA-BISSAU
Vaccines: Hepatitis A, polio, tetanus, yellow fever
Ls/local: Typhoid; consider BCG, diphtheria, hepatitis B, meningococcal A&C, rabies
Malaria: All areas; high risk; year round; chloroquine resistance reported
Prophylaxis: MEF (CHL + PRO)

GUYANA
Vaccines: Hepatitis A, polio, tetanus, yellow fever
Ls/local: Typhoid; consider BCG, diphtheria, hepatitis B, rabies
Malaria: Interior areas; risk exists; year round; chloroquine resistance reported
Prophylaxis: MEF (CHL + PRO)
Coastal areas, including Georgetown; low risk
No prophylaxis, avoid mosquito bites

HAITI

Vaccines: Hepatitis A, polio, tetanus
Ls/local: Typhoid; consider BCG, diphtheria, hepatitis B, rabies
Malaria: Suburban and rural areas below 300 m; risk exists; year round; no chloroquine resistance
Prophylaxis in risk areas: CHL (PRO)

HONDURAS

Vaccines: Hepatitis A, polio, tetanus
Ls/local: Typhoid; consider BCG, diphtheria, hepatitis B, rabies
Malaria: Rural areas; risk exists; year round; no chloroquine resistance
Prophylaxis in risk areas: CHL (PRO)

HONG KONG

Vaccines: Hepatitis A, polio, tetanus
Ls/local: Typhoid; consider BCG, diphtheria, hepatitis B, rabies

INDIA

Vaccines: Hepatitis A, polio, tetanus, typhoid
Ls/local: Consider BCG, diphtheria, hepatitis B, Japanese encephalitis, rabies
Malaria: Mountainous areas of Himachal Pradesh, Jammu and Kashmir, and Sikkim; no risk
No prophylaxis, avoid mosquito bites
All other areas; risk exists; year round; chloroquine resistance reported
Prophylaxis: CHL + PRO (MEF)

INDONESIA

Vaccines: Hepatitis A, polio, tetanus
Ls/local: Typhoid; consider BCG, diphtheria, hepatitis B, Japanese encephalitis, rabies
Malaria: Most areas; risk exists; year round; chloroquine resistance reported
Prophylaxis: CHL + PRO (MEF)
Irian Jaya; risk exists; year round; high chloroquine resistance
Prophylaxis: MEF (DOX)
Tourist resorts of Bali and Java and major cities; low risk
No prophylaxis, avoid mosquito bites

IRAN

Vaccines: Hepatitis A, polio, tetanus
Ls/local: Typhoid; consider BCG, diphtheria, hepatitis B, rabies
Malaria: Major cities; low risk
No prophylaxis, avoid mosquito bites
Most other areas; risk exists (greatest in south); March to November; chloroquine resistance reported
Prophylaxis: CHL + PRO (MEF)

IRAQ

Vaccines: Hepatitis A, polio, tetanus
Ls/local: Typhoid; consider BCG, diphtheria, hepatitis B, rabies
Malaria: Northern areas below 1500 m; risk exists; May to November; no chloroquine resistance
Prophylaxis in risk areas: CHL (PRO)

ISRAEL

Vaccines: Polio, tetanus
Ls/local: Hepatitis A, typhoid; consider BCG, diphtheria, hepatitis B, rabies

IVORY COAST

Vaccines: Hepatitis A, polio, tetanus, yellow fever
Ls/local: Typhoid; consider BCG, diphtheria, hepatitis B, meningococcal A&C, rabies
Malaria: All areas; high risk; year round; chloroquine resistance
Prophylaxis: MEF (CHL + PRO)

JAMAICA

Vaccines: Hepatitis A, polio, tetanus
Ls/local: Typhoid; consider BCG, diphtheria, hepatitis B

JAPAN

Vaccines: Polio, tetanus
Ls/local: Consider Japanese encephalitis

JORDAN

Vaccines: Hepatitis A, polio, tetanus
Ls/local: Typhoid; consider BCG, diphtheria, hepatitis B, rabies

KAMPUCHEA *see* CAMBODIA

KAZAKSTAN

Vaccines: Diphtheria, hepatitis A, polio, tetanus
Ls/local: Typhoid; consider BCG, hepatitis B, rabies

KENYA

Vaccines: Hepatitis A, polio, tetanus, yellow fever
Ls/local: Typhoid; consider BCG, diphtheria, hepatitis B, meningococcal A&C, rabies
Malaria: The city of Nairobi and above 2500 m; low risk
No prophylaxis, avoid mosquito bites
All other areas; high risk; year round; high chloroquine resistance
Prophylaxis: MEF (CHL + PRO)

KIRIBATI

Vaccines: Hepatitis A, polio, tetanus
Ls/local: Typhoid; consider BCG, diphtheria, hepatitis B

KOREA (North and South)
Vaccines: Hepatitis A, polio, tetanus
Ls/local: Typhoid; consider BCG, diphtheria, hepatitis B, Japanese encephalitis, rabies

KUWAIT
Vaccines: Hepatitis A, polio, tetanus
Ls/local: Typhoid; consider BCG, diphtheria, hepatitis B

KYRGYZSTAN
Vaccines: Diphtheria, hepatitis A, polio, tetanus
Ls/local: Typhoid; consider BCG, hepatitis B, rabies

LAOS
Vaccines: Hepatitis A, polio, tetanus
Ls/local: Typhoid; consider BCG, diphtheria, hepatitis B, Japanese encephalitis, rabies
Malaria: Vientiane; low risk
No prophylaxis, avoid mosquito bites
All other areas; risk exists; year round; high chloroquine resistance
Prophylaxis: MEF (DOX)

LATVIA
Vaccines: Diphtheria, hepatitis A, polio, tetanus
Ls/local: Typhoid; consider BCG, hepatitis B, rabies

LEBANON
Vaccines: Hepatitis A, polio, tetanus
Ls/local: Typhoid; consider BCG, diphtheria, hepatitis B, rabies

LESOTHO
Vaccines: Hepatitis A, polio, tetanus
Ls/local: Typhoid; consider BCG, diphtheria, hepatitis B, rabies

LIBERIA
Vaccines: Hepatitis A, polio, tetanus, yellow fever
Ls/local: Typhoid; consider BCG, diphtheria, hepatitis B, meningococcal A&C, rabies
Malaria: All areas; high risk; year round; high chloroquine resistance
Prophylaxis: MEF (CHL + PRO)

LIBYAN ARAB JAMAHIRIYA
Vaccines: Hepatitis A, polio, tetanus
Ls/local: Typhoid; consider BCG, diphtheria, hepatitis B, rabies
Malaria: Southwest; limited risk; February to August
No prophylaxis, avoid mosquito bites

LITHUANIA
Vaccines: Diphtheria, hepatitis A, polio, tetanus
Ls/local: Typhoid; consider BCG, hepatitis B, rabies

MACAO

Vaccines: Hepatitis A, polio, tetanus
Ls/local: Typhoid; consider BCG, diphtheria, hepatitis B, rabies

MADAGASCAR

Vaccines: Hepatitis A, polio, tetanus
Ls/local: Typhoid; consider BCG, diphtheria, hepatitis B, rabies
Malaria: All areas; high risk; year round; chloroquine resistance reported
Prophylaxis: MEF (CHL + PRO)

MALAWI

Vaccines: Hepatitis A, polio, tetanus
Ls/local: Typhoid; consider BCG, diphtheria, hepatitis B, meningococcal A&C, rabies
Malaria: High risk; all areas, year round; high chloroquine resistance
Prophylaxis: MEF (CHL + PRO)

MALAYSIA

Vaccines: Hepatitis A, polio, tetanus
Ls/local: Typhoid; consider BCG, diphtheria, hepatitis B, Japanese encephalitis, rabies
Malaria: Inland forested areas; some risk; year round; chloroquine resistance reported
Prophylaxis: CHL + PRO (MEF)
Sabah; risk exists; year round; high chloroquine resistance
Prophylaxis: MEF (CHL + PRO)
Urban and coastal areas, except in Sabah; no risk
No prophylaxis, avoid mosquito bites

MALDIVES

Vaccines: Hepatitis A, polio, tetanus
Ls/local: Typhoid; consider BCG, diphtheria, hepatitis B, rabies
Malaria: All areas; risk disappearing, last reported cases in 1983
No prophylaxis, avoid mosquito bites

MALI

Vaccines: Hepatitis A, polio, tetanus, yellow fever
Ls/local: Typhoid; consider BCG, diphtheria, hepatitis B, meningococcal A&C, rabies
Malaria: All areas; high risk; year round; chloroquine resistance reported
Prophylaxis: MEF (CHL + PRO)

MARSHALL ISLANDS

Vaccines: Hepatitis A, polio, tetanus
Ls/local: Typhoid; consider BCG, diphtheria, hepatitis B

MARTINIQUE

Vaccines: Hepatitis A, polio, tetanus
Ls/local: Typhoid; consider BCG, diphtheria, hepatitis B

MAURITANIA
Vaccines: Hepatitis A, polio, tetanus, yellow fever
Ls/local: Typhoid; consider BCG, diphtheria, hepatitis B, meningococcal A&C, rabies
Malaria: Dakhlet-Nouadhibou and Tiris-Zemour in the north; no risk
No prophylaxis; avoid mosquito bites
Adrar and Inchiri; risk exists; July to October (rainy season)
Prophylaxis: CHL + PRO (MEF)
All other areas; risk exists; year round
Prophylaxis: CHL + PRO (MEF)

MAURITIUS
Vaccines: Hepatitis A, polio, tetanus
Ls/local: Typhoid; consider BCG, diphtheria, hepatitis B
Malaria: Some rural areas only; risk exists; year round; no chloroquine resistance
No prophylaxis, avoid mosquito bites

MAYOTTE
Vaccines: Hepatitis A, polio, tetanus
Ls/local: Typhoid; consider BCG, diphtheria, hepatitis B, rabies
Malaria: All areas; high risk; year round
Prophylaxis: MEF (CHL + PRO)

MEXICO
Vaccines: Hepatitis A, polio, tetanus
Ls/local: Typhoid; consider BCG, diphtheria, hepatitis B, rabies
Malaria: Some rural areas rarely visited by tourists; risk exists; year round; no chloroquine resistance
Prophylaxis: CHL (PRO)
All other areas; no risk
No prophylaxis, avoid mosquito bites

MICRONESIA
Vaccines: Hepatitis A, polio, tetanus
Ls/local: Typhoid; consider BCG, diphtheria, hepatitis B

MOLDOVA
Vaccines: Diphtheria, hepatitis A, polio, tetanus
Ls/local: Typhoid; consider BCG, hepatitis B, rabies

MONGOLIA
Vaccines: Hepatitis A, polio, tetanus
Ls/local: Diphtheria, typhoid; consider BCG, hepatitis B, rabies

MOROCCO
Vaccines: Hepatitis A, polio, tetanus
Ls/local: Typhoid; consider BCG, diphtheria, hepatitis B, rabies
Malaria: Some rural areas only; limited risk; May to October; no chloroquine resistance
No prophylaxis, avoid mosquito bites

MOZAMBIQUE
Vaccines: Hepatitis A, polio, tetanus
Ls/local: Typhoid; consider BCG, diphtheria, hepatitis B, meningococcal A&C, rabies
Malaria: All areas; high risk; year round; chloroquine resistance
Prophylaxis: MEF (CHL + PRO)

MYANMAR
Vaccines: Hepatitis A, polio, tetanus
Ls/local: Typhoid; consider BCG, diphtheria, hepatitis B, Japanese encephalitis, rabies
Malaria: All areas; risk exists; year round; high chloroquine resistance
Prophylaxis: MEF (DOX)

NAMIBIA
Vaccines: Hepatitis A, polio, tetanus
Ls/local: Typhoid; consider BCG, diphtheria, hepatitis B, rabies
Malaria: Along the Kavango river; risk exists; year round; chloroquine resistance reported
Prophylaxis: CHL + PRO (MEF)
Northern regions; risk exists; November to June; chloroquine resistance reported
Prophylaxis: CHL + PRO (MEF)
All other areas; low risk
No prophylaxis, avoid mosquito bites

NEPAL
Vaccines: Hepatitis A, polio, tetanus, typhoid
Ls/local. Consider BCG, diphtheria, hepatitis B, Japanese encephalitis, meningococcal A&C, rabies
Malaria: Rural areas below 1300 m, including Terai district; risk exists; year round; chloroquine resistance reported
Prophylaxis: CHL + PRO (MEF)
All other areas, including Katmandu; no or low risk
No prophylaxis, avoid mosquito bites

NEW CALEDONIA AND DEPENDENCIES
Vaccines: Hepatitis A, polio, tetanus
Ls/local: Typhoid; consider BCG, diphtheria, hepatitis B

NEW INDEPENDENT STATES OF THE FORMER SOVIET UNION *see* ARMENIA, AZERBAIJAN, BELARUS, ESTONIA, GEORGIA, KAZAKSTAN, KYRGYZSTAN, LATVIA, LITHUANIA, MOLDOVA, RUSSIAN FEDERATION, TAJIKISTAN, TURKMENISTAN, UKRAINE, UZBEKISTAN

NICARAGUA
Vaccines: Hepatitis A, polio, tetanus
Ls/local: Typhoid; consider BCG, diphtheria, hepatitis B, rabies
Malaria: Rural areas and outskirts of cities; risk exists; June to December; no chloroquine resistance
Prophylaxis in risk areas: CHL (PRO)

NIGER
Vaccines: Hepatitis A, polio, tetanus, yellow fever
Ls/local: Typhoid; consider BCG, diphtheria, hepatitis B, meningococcal A&C, rabies
Malaria: All areas; high risk; year round; chloroquine resistance reported
Prophylaxis: MEF (CHL + PRO)

NIGERIA
Vaccines: Hepatitis A, polio, tetanus, yellow fever
Ls/local: Typhoid; consider BCG, diphtheria, hepatitis B, meningococcal A&C, rabies
Malaria: All areas; high risk; year round; chloroquine resistance reported
Prophylaxis: MEF (CHL + PRO)

OMAN
Vaccines: Hepatitis A, polio, tetanus
Ls/local: Typhoid; consider BCG, diphtheria, hepatitis B, rabies
Malaria: Above 2000 m and in desert areas; no risk
No prophylaxis, avoid mosquito bites
All other areas; risk exists; year round; chloroquine resistance reported
Prophylaxis: CHL + PRO (MEF)

PACIFIC ISLANDS (Trust Territory of the USA)
Vaccines: Hepatitis A, polio, tetanus
Ls/local: Typhoid; consider BCG, diphtheria, hepatitis B

PAKISTAN
Vaccines: Hepatitis A, polio, tetanus, typhoid
Ls/local: Consider BCG, diphtheria, hepatitis B, Japanese encephalitis, rabies
Malaria: Below 2000 m; risk exists; year round; chloroquine resistance reported
Prophylaxis in risk areas: CHL + PRO (MEF)

PANAMA
Vaccines: Hepatitis A, polio, tetanus, yellow fever (for travellers going to the Province of Darien)
Ls/local: Typhoid; consider BCG, diphtheria, hepatitis B, rabies
Malaria: Rural areas; risk exists; year round; chloroquine resistance reported
Prophylaxis in risk areas: CHL (PRO)

PAPUA NEW GUINEA
Vaccines: Hepatitis A, polio, tetanus
Ls/local: Typhoid; consider BCG, diphtheria, hepatitis B
Malaria: Below 1800 m; high risk; year round; chloroquine resistance reported
Prophylaxis in risk areas: MEF (DOX)

PARAGUAY
Vaccines: Hepatitis A, polio, tetanus
Ls/local: Typhoid; consider BCG, diphtheria, hepatitis B, rabies
Malaria: Rural areas, risk exists; October to May; no chloroquine resistance
Prophylaxis in risk areas: CHL (PRO)

PERU
Vaccines: Hepatitis A, polio, tetanus, yellow fever
Ls/local: Typhoid; consider BCG, diphtheria, hepatitis B, rabies
Malaria: Rural areas below 1500 m; risk exists; year round; chloroquine resistance reported
Prophylaxis: CHL + PRO (MEF)
All other areas, including urban areas and above 1500 m; low risk
No prophylaxis, avoid mosquito bites

PHILIPPINES
Vaccines: Hepatitis A, polio, tetanus
Ls/local: Typhoid; consider BCG, diphtheria, hepatitis B, Japanese encephalitis, rabies
Malaria: Rural areas below 600 m; risk exists; year round; chloroquine resistance reported
Prophylaxis: CHL + PRO (MEF)
All other areas, including Bohol, Catanduanes, Cebu and urban areas such as Manila; no risk
No prophylaxis, avoid mosquito bites

PUERTO RICO
Vaccines: Hepatitis A, polio, tetanus
Ls/local: Typhoid; consider BCG, diphtheria, hepatitis B, rabies

QATAR
Vaccines: Hepatitis A, polio, tetanus
Ls/local: Typhoid; consider BCG, diphtheria, hepatitis B, rabies

REUNION
Vaccines: Hepatitis A, polio, tetanus
Ls/local: Typhoid; consider BCG, diphtheria, hepatitis B

ROMANIA
Vaccines: Hepatitis A, polio, tetanus
Ls/local: Diphtheria, typhoid; consider BCG, hepatitis B, rabies

RUSSIAN FEDERATION
Vaccines: Diphtheria, hepatitis A, polio, tetanus
Ls/local: Typhoid; consider BCG, hepatitis B, rabies

RWANDA
Vaccines: Hepatitis A, polio, tetanus, yellow fever
Ls/local: Typhoid; consider BCG, diphtheria, hepatitis B, meningococcal A&C, rabies
Malaria: All areas; high risk; year round; high chloroquine resistance
Prophylaxis: MEF (CHL + PRO)

SAINT HELENA
Vaccines: Hepatitis A, polio, tetanus
Ls/local: Typhoid; consider BCG, diphtheria, hepatitis B

SAINT KITTS AND NEVIS
Vaccines: Hepatitis A, polio, tetanus
Ls/local: Typhoid; consider BCG, diphtheria, hepatitis B

SAINT LUCIA
Vaccines: Hepatitis A, polio, tetanus
Ls/local: Typhoid; consider BCG, diphtheria, hepatitis B

SAINT VINCENT AND THE GRENADINES
Vaccines: Hepatitis A, polio, tetanus
Ls/local: Typhoid; consider BCG, diphtheria, hepatitis B

SAMOA
Vaccines: Hepatitis A, polio, tetanus
Ls/local: Typhoid; consider BCG, diphtheria, hepatitis B

SAO TOME AND PRINCIPE
Vaccines: Hepatitis A, polio, tetanus, yellow fever
Ls/local: Typhoid; consider BCG, diphtheria, hepatitis B, rabies
Malaria: All areas; high risk; year round; chloroquine resistance reported
Prophylaxis: MEF (CHL + PRO)

SAUDI ARABIA
Vaccines: Hepatitis A, polio, tetanus
Ls/local: Typhoid; consider BCG, diphtheria, hepatitis B, meningococcal A&C, rabies
NOTE: All those on the Hajj pilgrimage to Mecca must have meningococcal A&C vaccine at least 10 days before travel. A certificate of vaccination is required; this is valid for 3 years
Malaria: Urban areas of Western Province (Jeddah, Mecca, Medina, Taif), eastern, northern and central provinces and the high altitude areas of Asir Plateau; low risk
No prophylaxis, avoid mosquito bites
All other areas; risk exists; year round; chloroquine resistance reported
Prophylaxis: CHL + PRO (MEF)

SENEGAL
Vaccines: Hepatitis A, polio, tetanus, yellow fever
Ls/local: Typhoid; consider BCG, diphtheria, hepatitis B, meningococcal A&C, rabies
Malaria: All areas; high risk; year round; chloroquine resistance reported
Prophylaxis: MEF (CHL + PRO)

SEYCHELLES
Vaccines: Hepatitis A, polio, tetanus
Ls/local: Typhoid; consider BCG, diphtheria, hepatitis B

SIERRA LEONE
Vaccines: Hepatitis A, polio, tetanus, yellow fever
Ls/local: Typhoid; consider BCG, diphtheria, hepatitis B, meningococcal A&C, rabies
Malaria: All areas; high risk; year round; chloroquine resistance reported
Prophylaxis: MEF (CHL + PRO)

SINGAPORE
Vaccines: Hepatitis A, polio, tetanus
Ls/local: Typhoid; consider BCG, diphtheria, hepatitis B, rabies

SLOVAKIA
Vaccines: Hepatitis A, polio, tetanus
Ls/local: Diphtheria, typhoid; consider BCG, hepatitis B, rabies

SLOVENIA
Vaccines: Hepatitis A, polio, tetanus
Ls/local: Diphtheria, typhoid; consider BCG, hepatitis B, rabies

SOLOMON ISLANDS

Vaccines: Hepatitis A, polio, tetanus
Ls/local: Typhoid; consider BCG, diphtheria, hepatitis B
Malaria: A few eastern and southern islets; no risk
No prophylaxis, avoid mosquito bites
All other areas; high risk; year round; chloroquine resistance reported
Prophylaxis: MEF (DOX)

SOMALIA

Vaccines: Hepatitis A, polio, tetanus, yellow fever
Ls/local: Typhoid; consider BCG, diphtheria, hepatitis B, meningococcal A&C, rabies
Malaria: All areas; high risk; year round; chloroquine resistance reported
Prophylaxis: MEF (CHL + PRO)

SOUTH AFRICA

Vaccines: Hepatitis A, polio, tetanus
Ls/local: Typhoid; consider BCG, diphtheria, hepatitis B, rabies
Malaria: Low altitude areas of the northern and eastern Transvaal, including the Kruger National Park and north-eastern Kwazulu/Natal as far south as the Tugela river; risk exists; year round; chloroquine resistance reported
Prophylaxis: CHL + PRO (MEF)
All other areas, including Cape Town, Port Elizabeth, Durban and Johannesburg; little or no risk
No prophylaxis, avoid mosquito bites

SRI LANKA

Vaccines: Hepatitis A, polio, tetanus, typhoid
Ls/local: Consider BCG, diphtheria, hepatitis B, Japanese encephalitis, rabies
Malaria: District of Colombo, Kalutara and Nuwara Eliya; low risk
No prophylaxis, avoid mosquito bites
All other areas; risk exists; year round; chloroquine resistance reported
Prophylaxis: CHL + PRO (MEF)

SUDAN

Vaccines: Hepatitis A, polio, tetanus, yellow fever
Ls/local: Typhoid; consider BCG, diphtheria, hepatitis B, meningococcal A&C, rabies
Malaria: All areas; high risk; year round; high chloroquine resistance
Prophylaxis: MEF (CHL + PRO)

SURINAM
Vaccines: Hepatitis A, polio, tetanus, yellow fever
Ls/local: Typhoid; consider BCG, diphtheria, hepatitis B, rabies
Malaria: Paramaribo District and coastal areas; low risk
No prophylaxis, avoid mosquito bites
All other areas; risk exists; year round; high chloroquine resistance
Prophylaxis: MEF (CHL + PRO)

SWAZILAND
Vaccines: Hepatitis A, polio, tetanus
Ls/local: Typhoid; consider BCG, diphtheria, hepatitis B, rabies
Malaria: Low veld areas; high risk; year round; high chloroquine resistance
Prophylaxis in risk areas: MEF (CHL + PRO)

SYRIAN ARAB REPUBLIC
Vaccines: Hepatitis A, polio, tetanus
Ls/local: Typhoid; consider BCG, diphtheria, hepatitis B, rabies
Malaria: Northern border areas; risk exists; May to October; no chloroquine resistance
Prophylaxis in risk areas: CHL (PRO)

TAIWAN
Vaccines: Hepatitis A, polio, tetanus
Ls/local: Typhoid; consider BCG, diphtheria, hepatitis B, Japanese encephalitis

TAJIKISTAN
Vaccines: Diphtheria, hepatitis A, polio, tetanus
Ls/local: Typhoid; consider BCG, hepatitis B, rabies
Malaria: Southern border areas; risk exists; year round; no chloroquine resistance
Prophylaxis in risk areas: CHL (PRO)

TANZANIA
Vaccines: Hepatitis A, polio, tetanus, yellow fever
Ls/local: Typhoid; consider BCG, diphtheria, hepatitis B, meningococcal A&C, rabies
Malaria: Below 1800 m; high risk; year round; high chloroquine resistance
Prophylaxis in risk areas: MEF (CHL + PRO)

COUNTRY GUIDELINES

THAILAND

Vaccines: Hepatitis A, polio, tetanus
Ls/local: Typhoid; consider BCG, diphtheria, hepatitis B, Japanese encephalitis, rabies
Malaria: Rural areas, especially in forested and hilly areas; risk exists; year round; high chloroquine resistance
For day trips: no prophylaxis, avoid mosquito bites
For longer trips: prophylaxis: MEF (DOX)
Border areas with Cambodia (Kampuchea) and Myanmar (Burma): risk exists; year round; mefloquine resistance reported
Prophylaxis: DOX (MEF)
All other areas, including cities and main tourist resorts of Bangkok, Chiangmai, Pattaya, Phuket and islands; low risk
No prophylaxis, avoid mosquito bites

TOGO

Vaccines: Hepatitis A, polio, tetanus, yellow fever
Ls/local: Typhoid; consider BCG, diphtheria, hepatitis B, meningococcal A&C, rabies
Malaria: All areas; high risk; year round; chloroquine resistance reported
Prophylaxis: MEF (CHL + PRO)

TONGA

Vaccines: Hepatitis A, polio, tetanus
Ls/local: Typhoid; consider BCG, diphtheria, hepatitis B

TRINIDAD AND TOBAGO

Vaccines: Hepatitis A, polio, tetanus
Ls/local: Typhoid; consider BCG, diphtheria, hepatitis B, rabies
NOTE: Travellers sometimes make trips to mainland South America and thus need yellow fever vaccination and may need antimalarials

TUNISIA

Vaccines: Hepatitis A, polio, tetanus
Ls/local: Typhoid; consider BCG, diphtheria, hepatitis B, rabies

TURKEY

Vaccines: Hepatitis A, polio, tetanus
Ls/local: Typhoid; consider BCG, diphtheria, hepatitis B, rabies
Malaria: Southeast Anatolia and the Cukurova/Amikova areas; risk exists; March to November; no chloroquine resistance
Prophylaxis: CHL (PRO)
All other areas, including tourist areas; low risk
No prophylaxis, avoid mosquito bites

TURKMENISTAN

Vaccines: Diphtheria, hepatitis A, polio, tetanus
Ls/local: Typhoid; consider BCG, hepatitis B, rabies
Malaria: Border with Afghanistan; a few cases have been reported
No prophylaxis, avoid mosquito bites

UGANDA

Vaccines: Hepatitis A, polio, tetanus, yellow fever
Ls/local: Typhoid; consider BCG, diphtheria, hepatitis B, meningococcal A&C, rabies
Malaria: All areas; high risk; year round; chloroquine resistance reported
Prophylaxis: MEF (CHL + PRO)

UKRAINE

Vaccines: Diphtheria, hepatitis A, polio, tetanus
Ls/local: Typhoid; consider BCG, hepatitis B, rabies

UNITED ARAB EMIRATES

Vaccines: Hepatitis A, polio, tetanus
Ls/local: Typhoid; consider BCG, diphtheria, hepatitis B, rabies
Malaria: Foothill areas and valleys of the northern Emirates; risk exists; year round
Prophylaxis: CHL + PRO (MEF)
All other areas, including Abu Dhabi, Dubai, Sharjah, Ajman and Umm al Qaiwain; no risk
No prophylaxis, avoid mosquito bites

URUGUAY

Vaccines: Hepatitis A, polio, tetanus
Ls/local: Typhoid; consider BCG, diphtheria, hepatitis B, rabies

UZBEKISTAN

Vaccines: Diphtheria, hepatitis A, polio, tetanus
Ls/local: Typhoid; consider BCG, hepatitis B, rabies

VANUATU

Vaccines: Hepatitis A, polio, tetanus
Ls/local: Typhoid; consider BCG, diphtheria, hepatitis B
Malaria: Futuna Island; no risk
No prophylaxis, avoid mosquito bites
All other areas; high risk; year round; high chloroquine resistance
Prophylaxis: MEF (DOX)

VENEZUELA

Vaccines: Hepatitis A, polio, tetanus, yellow fever
Ls/local: Typhoid; consider BCG, diphtheria, hepatitis B, rabies
NOTE: Yellow fever vaccine is not required for visits to Margarita Island only

Malaria: Most rural areas, including Angel Falls; risk exists; year round; chloroquine resistance reported
For day trips: no prophylaxis, avoid mosquito bites
For longer trips: prophylaxis: CHL + PRO (MEF)
Amazon basin region; risk exists; year round; high chloroquine resistance
Prophylaxis: MEF (CHL + PRO)
Urban areas, including Caracus; low risk
No prophylaxis, avoid mosquito bites
Margarita Island; no risk
No prophylaxis, avoid mosquito bites

VIETNAM

Vaccines: Hepatitis A, polio, tetanus
Ls/local: Typhoid; consider BCG, diphtheria, hepatitis B, Japanese encephalitis, rabies

Malaria: Cities and Red River delta; low risk
No prophylaxis, avoid mosquito bites
All other areas; risk exists; year round; high chloroquine resistance
Prophylaxis: MEF (DOX)

VIRGIN ISLANDS

Vaccines: Hepatitis A, polio, tetanus
Ls/local: Typhoid; consider BCG, diphtheria, hepatitis B

WEST INDIES *see* ANTIGUA AND BARBUDA, BAHAMAS, BARBADOS, BRITISH VIRGIN ISLANDS, CAYMAN ISLANDS, DOMINICA, DOMINICAN REPUBLIC, GRENADA, GRENADINES, GUADELOUPE, HAITI, JAMAICA, MARTINIQUE, PUERTO RICO, SAINT HELENA, SAINT KITTS–NEVIS, SAINT LUCIA, SAINT VINCENT, TRINIDAD AND TOBAGO, VIRGIN ISLANDS

YEMEN

Vaccines: Hepatitis A, polio, tetanus
Ls/local: Typhoid; consider BCG, diphtheria, hepatitis B, rabies

Malaria: Aden; no or low risk
No prophylaxis, avoid mosquito bites
All other areas; risk exists; September to February; chloroquine resistance reported
Prophylaxis: CHL + PRO (MEF)

YUGOSLAVIA

Vaccines: Hepatitis A, polio, tetanus
Ls/local: Typhoid; consider BCG, diphtheria, hepatitis B, rabies

ZAIRE
Vaccines: Hepatitis A, polio, tetanus, yellow fever
Ls/local: Typhoid; consider BCG, diphtheria, hepatitis B, meningococcal A&C, rabies
Malaria: All areas; high risk; year round; high chloroquine resistance
Prophylaxis: MEF (CHL + PRO)

ZAMBIA
Vaccines: Hepatitis A, polio, tetanus, yellow fever
Ls/local: Typhoid; consider BCG, diphtheria, hepatitis B, meningococcal A&C, rabies
Malaria: All areas; high risk; year round; high chloroquine resistance
Prophylaxis: MEF (CHL + PRO)

ZIMBABWE
Vaccines: Hepatitis A, polio, tetanus
Ls/local: Typhoid; consider BCG, diphtheria, hepatitis B, rabies
Malaria: Zambezi valley, including Victoria Falls; risk exists; year round; chloroquine resistance reported
Prophylaxis: MEF (CHL + PRO)
Below 1200 m; risk exists; November to June; chloroquine resistance reported
Prophylaxis: MEF (CHL + PRO)
Above 1200 m, including Harare and Bulawayo; low risk
No prophylaxis, avoid mosquito bites

APPENDIX II: VACCINE GUIDELINES

A summary of travellers' vaccines are given in alphabetical order of disease, with guidelines for use. More extensive information about these vaccines and the practice of immunization can be found in the literature *(see Immunisation against Infectious Diseases [Appendix III])*.

For full details on contraindications, side effects and dosage schedules, please consult the manufacturers' data sheet.

Anaphylaxis

Anaphylaxis, although rare, can occur after vaccination. Health staff giving vaccines must be able to recognise and treat anaphylaxis. Essential items to treat it must always be immediately to hand, including adrenaline, needle, syringe and airway. For further details on the management of anaphylaxis, refer to the literature (*see Immunisation against Infectious Diseases [Appendix III]*).

CHOLERA

Transmission: Faecal–oral route, usually through contaminated water and food, particularly shellfish

Risk areas: Countries where food and water are liable to faecal contamination, especially the Indian subcontinent, Asia, Africa and Central and South America

Recommendations: The risk of acquiring cholera is very low for travellers, thus, cholera vaccination is not recommended.

Those who need effective immunity, such as health workers going to refugee or emergency situations where hygiene is difficult, may benefit from the full two-dose schedule *(see manufacturers' data sheet)* or one of the new oral cholera vaccines, when these become available.

Vaccine: Inactivated cholera vaccine *(currently unavailable in the UK)*
Storage: 2–8°C; do not freeze

Schedule:

Dosage	Adults and children >1 year 0.1 ml, intradermally
Primary course	One dose only if evidence of vaccination is required; the statement of vaccination is valid for 6 months; vaccinations confer minimal protection
Duration of protection	Valid (but not effective) for 6 months
Booster	After 6 months, if evidence of vaccination is required

Pregnancy: Not recommended

Children: Not recommended in children aged less than 1 year

Contraindications: Acute febrile illness, severe reaction to previous vaccine, pregnancy

Side effects:
Local: pain, erythema, swelling
General: fever, malaise, headache

Notes:
Repeated vaccination may result in the development of hypersensitivity.

The current injectable cholera vaccine gives only limited personal protection and does not prevent spread of the disease. The 1973 World Health Assembly stated that cholera vaccination should no longer be required of any traveller. In remote areas, border officials may occasionally ask to see certificates of people travelling from an infected area; such travellers are advised to carry a statement of the International Health Regulations on official notepaper, signed and stamped by a medical practitioner. Alternatively, if vaccine is available, they can be given a single dose of vaccine only to prevent the risk of having an injection abroad. No official vaccination certificate is available.

DIPHTHERIA

Transmission: Droplet infection and through contact with soiled clothes or with a carrier

Risk areas: Worldwide, especially the New Independent States of the former USSR, where epidemics of diphtheria are occurring: 47 261 reported cases in 1994, continuing to rise through 1995; also common in many developing countries

Recommendations: All individuals should have received a primary course of vaccination.

We encourage all travellers aged more than 10 years to have a booster dose with combined low-dose diphtheria–tetanus vaccine when a tetanus booster is needed. Many adults in the UK have been found to have a poor level of immunity to diphtheria.
Children should always be up-to-date with diphtheria vaccination.

High-risk groups: Travellers who will come into close contact with local people for prolonged periods, in the New Independent States of the former USSR and in developing countries; a booster dose at 10-year intervals is recommended

Vaccine: Inactivated diphtheria toxoid vaccine (low-dose adsorbed diphtheria–tetanus vaccine; Diphtheria Vaccine Adults, low-dose adsorbed diphtheria vaccine)
Storage: 2–8°C; do not freeze

Schedule:	
Dosage	Adults and children > 10 years 0.5 ml, subcutaneously; low-dose diphtheria–tetanus or diphtheria vaccine
Primary course	Three doses, with a 4-week interval between each dose (most people receive this in childhood)
Effective	After third dose
Duration of protection	10 years
Booster	One dose 10-yearly

Pregnancy: Not recommended

Children: Safe; higher-dose vaccine available for children aged less than 10 years; most children receive the vaccine with the routine childhood vaccinations

Contraindications: Acute febrile illness, severe reaction to previous vaccine. Combined low-dose diphtheria–tetanus vaccine should not be given if the person has received tetanus vaccine in the past 10 years

Side effects:
Local: swelling, redness, nodule (may persist for months) at injection site
General: transient fever, malaise, headache

Notes:

The full dose of the childhood diphtheria vaccine must not be given to adults and children aged more than 10 years. If no low-dose diphtheria vaccine is available for a high-risk traveller, the Chief Medical Officer suggests giving one-fifth (0.1 ml) of the monovalent child diphtheria vaccine by deep subcutaneous injection *(unlicensed use; consult a specialist)*

Routine vaccination against diphtheria started in 1940 in the UK; most people have received a primary course of diphtheria vaccine.

People who have had diphtheria should still receive this vaccine because the illness does not confer immunity.

HEPATITIS A

Transmission: Faecal–oral route, usually by ingestion of contaminated food or water

Risk areas: Present throughout the world, but the risk varies widely, being much higher in countries where food and water are liable to faecal contamination

High-risk: Asia (particularly high in the Indian subcontinent), Africa, Central and South America, the Middle East, the New Independent States of the former USSR, the Dominican Republic and Haiti

Moderate-risk: Turkey and most Caribbean islands

Low-risk: North, south and west Europe, North America, Australia and New Zealand

Recommendations: All travellers to medium- and high-risk areas should be considered for vaccination

Vaccine: Inactivated hepatitis A vaccine; junior version available for children aged 1–15 years
Storage: 2–8°C; do not freeze

Immunoglobulin: Human normal immunoglobulin (HNIG), which contains hepatitis A antibodies
Storage: 2–8°C; do not freeze

Hepatitis A vaccine

Schedule:	
For travellers aged > 15 years	
Dosage	1 ml, intramuscular injection to deltoid muscle
Primary course	One dose
Effective	2 weeks after primary course
Duration of protection	After primary course, 1 year; after booster dose, 10 years
Booster	One dose 6–12 months after primary course
For travellers aged 1–15 years	
Dosage	0.5 ml, intramuscular injection to deltoid muscle
Primary course	One dose
Effective	2 weeks after primary course
Duration of protection	After primary course, 1 year; after booster dose, 10 years
Booster	One dose 6–12 months after primary course

Pregnancy: Not recommended

Children: Safe, can be given from age 1 year

Hepatitis A protection is not a priority for children aged less than 10 years because they tend to develop only a mild or asymptomatic illness. However, they may still excrete the virus and thus be a source of secondary cases. Giving hepatitis A protection to children may be worthwhile if they are likely to be in contact with people with no immunity to hepatitis A after return, for example through attendance at a day nursery. Hepatitis A protection should be given to children with immunosuppression

Contraindications: Acute febrile illness, severe reaction to previous vaccine

Side effects:
Local: mild soreness, erythema, induration
General: fever, malaise, fatigue, headache, anorexia

Notes:
Previous infection with hepatitis A makes vaccination unnecessary. When time allows, the antibody status of the following groups of people should be checked:

- Those aged more than 50 years
- Those who have lived in developing countries
- Those with a history of jaundice

The hepatitis A illness is more severe in older people.

Late-presenting regular travellers can be given both immunoglobulin and hepatitis A vaccine to infer both short- and long-term protection

Human normal immunoglobulin

This is not a vaccine

Schedule:	
Dosage	250 mg (2 ml); 500 mg (4 ml); deep intramuscular injection to gluteal muscle
Primary course	Single dose; repeat as required
Effective	After 24 h
Duration of protection	250 mg, 2 months; 500 mg, 4 months
Booster	Short-term protection only; repeat as required

Pregnancy: Safe

Children: Not recommended in children aged less than 1 year; in those aged more than 1 year dose must be adjusted by weight or age (*see manufacturers' data sheet)*

Contraindications: None

Side effects:
Generally very well tolerated. Always withdraw plunger and look for blood before injecting to avoid intravenous administration, which can lead to shock

Notes:
Human normal immunoglobulin is particularly useful for some travellers, such as pregnant women, immunosuppressed patients and last-minute travellers.

It does not inhibit the effect of yellow fever or oral typhoid vaccines and, when oral polio is being given as a booster dose, the effect is not likely to be significant, so it can be given at the same time as, or before, these vaccines if necessary. It can be given with any killed vaccine.

HEPATITIS B

Transmission: Parenteral spread through contaminated blood or blood products or by intimate sexual contact with an infected person

Risk areas: Worldwide (*see map*)

Recommendations: Certain groups are at increased risk of contracting hepatitis B. *High-risk groups:*

- Health workers
- Those planning to spend more than 6 months abroad in developing countries or the New Independent States of the former USSR
- Children who will be living in developing countries or the New Independent States of the former USSR
- Those who will be in contact with known carriers
- Those who place themselves at risk through their sexual behaviour or through intravenous drug abuse

Vaccine: Inactivated recombinant hepatitis BsAg vaccine
Storage: 2–8°C; do not freeze

Schedule:	
Dosage	Adults and children > 12 years* 1.0 ml, children < 12 years 0.5 ml. Intramuscular injection to deltoid muscle; the anterolateral thigh is preferred site for infants; do not give in buttock
Primary course	Three doses, at months 0,1 and 6. Rapid schedule: months 0, 1 and 2; must have booster at 1 year
Effective	2 months after third dose in 90% of vaccinees
Duration of protection	3–5 years
Booster	One dose every 3–5 years

Pregnancy: Recommended in women known to be at high risk

Children: Safe; can be given from birth

Contraindications: Severe febrile illness, severe reaction to previous vaccine

Side effects:
Local: pain, erythema
General: transient malaise, arthralgia, fever

Notes:
Health workers and others who need to be certain that they have immunity should have antibody levels checked 2–4 months after the full vaccination course.

Global distribution of hepatitis B infection

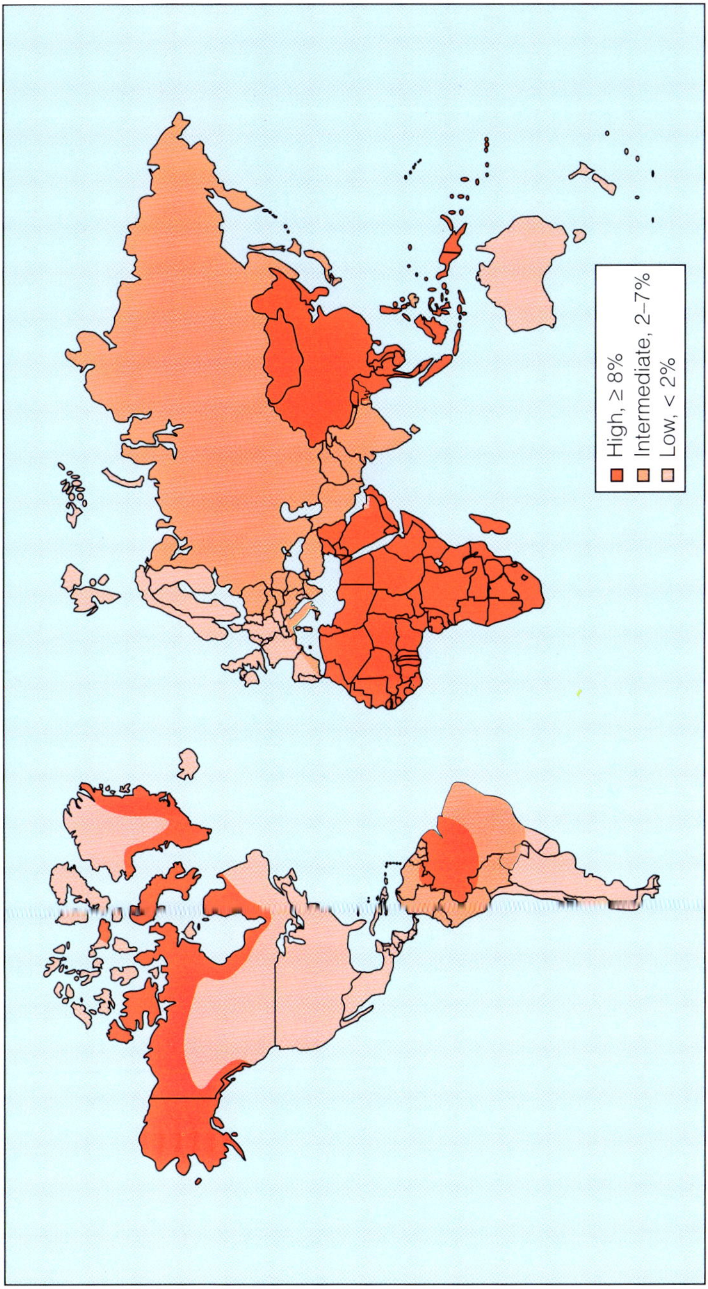

VACCINE GUIDELINES

JAPANESE ENCEPHALITIS

Transmission: Mosquito bites

Risk areas: Many areas of Asia, particularly after the rainy season in rural areas *(see table and map overleaf)*

Recommendations: The risk of travellers acquiring Japanese encephalitis is extremely low but travel to rural areas during the transmission season increases the risk. All travellers should be advised to avoid mosquito bites.

Consider the vaccine for those spending 1 month or longer in an endemic area during the transmission season, especially if travel will include excursions into rural areas. *For known areas of transmission see table and map.*

Vaccine: Inactivated vaccine, available only on a named-patient basis (*unlicensed in the UK*)
Storage: 2–8°C; do not freeze

Schedule:	
Dosage	Adults and children > 3 years 1 ml, children aged 1–3 years 0.5 ml, deep subcutaneous injection
Primary course	Three doses, on days 0, 7 and 30. Rapid schedule on days 0, 7 and 14 or two doses 1–4 weeks apart
Effective	1 month after full primary course
Duration of protection	At least 2 years in those who have completed full primary course. Rapid schedule confers immunity for about 3 months in 80% of vaccinees
Booster	One dose every 2–3 years (but little data available)

Pregnancy: Not recommended

Children: Not recommended in children aged less than 1 year

Contraindications: Severe febrile illness or other active infection, chronic heart, kidney or liver disease, diabetes, leukaemia, lymphoma, generalized malignant disease, severe reaction to previous vaccine, pregnancy

Side effects: *See notes below*
Local: induration, erythema, tenderness
Systemic: headache, fever, malaise, joint pains

Notes:
Young children, the elderly and pregnant women have a higher risk of contracting the illness.

Infection with Japanese encephalitis virus leads to severe encephalitis in fewer than 1% of those infected. Those who develop encephalitis have a high mortality and high rate of neuropsychiatric sequelae.

Reported reactions after vaccination include:

- Japan: encephalitis, encephalopathy, seizures, peripheral neuropathy; frequency 1–2.3 per million patients vaccinated

- Australia, Europe and North America: urticaria, angioedema of the extremities, occasional respiratory distress; frequency 1–100 per 10 000 patients vaccinated. Reactions have occurred up to 2 weeks after vaccination but 88% occurred within 3 days. These reactions have happened after uneventful first and second doses. An association has been established between these reactions and a previous history of urticaria. Vaccinated patients should be observed for 30 min after vaccination and warned about the possibility of adverse reactions. They should be advised to remain within ready access of medical care in the 10 days after receiving a dose of Japanese encephalitis vaccine.

Risk of Japanese encephalitis:

Country	Affected areas	Transmission season (main risk season)
Bangladesh	Little data, probably widespread	Possibly July to December
Bhutan	No data	No data
Brunei	Presumed widespread	Year round
Cambodia (Kampuchea)	All	Probably May to October
China	All except Xizang (Tibet), Xinjiang, Qinghai	North China; May to September South China; April to October
Hong Kong	Rare cases in new territories	April to October
India	All except Arunachal, Dadra, Daman Diu, Gujarat, Himachal, Jammu, Kashmir, Lakshadweep, Meghalaja, Nagar Haveli, Orissa, Punjab, Sikhim, Rajasthan	North India including Assam, Bihar, Manipure, West Bengal and Uttah Pradesh: July to December Andhra Pradesh: September to December Goa: May to October Karnataka: August to December Kerala: increased number of cases reported in early 1996 Mandya: April to June Tamilnadu: October to January
Indonesia	Most areas, including Bali	Probably year round; peak November to March, June to July.
Japan	Rare on all islands except Hokkaido. Risk present if involved in farm or stockraising activities in the summer	April to October
Korea	South Korea, all North Korea, no data	July to October
Laos	All	Probably May to October
Malaysia	Peninsula, Sarawak and probably Sabah	Year round

VACCINE GUIDELINES

Country	Affected areas	Transmission season (main risk season)
Myanmar (Burma)	All	Probably May to October
Nepal	Southern lowlands (Terai)	July to December
Pakistan	Central deltas	Probably June to January
Philippines	Probably on all islands	West Luzon, Mindoro, Negro Palowan; possibly April to November Elsewhere; year round; peak April to January
Russia	South of Khabarousk (Far eastern maritime area)	Peak July to September
Singapore	Rare in all areas	Year round; peak April
Sri Lanka	All except mountainous areas	October to January; May to June
Taiwan	All	April to October; peak June
Thailand	All, higher risk in north	May to October
Vietnam	All	May to October
Western Pacific	Guam, Saipan *(2 epidemics reported since 1947)*	Possibly September to January

Transmission patterns may change.
Local Japanese encephalitis incidence rates may not accurately reflect risks to non-immune travellers because of high immunization rates in local populations.
High levels of viral transmission may occur without human disease.

Areas of proven or suspected Japanese encephalitis virus transmission

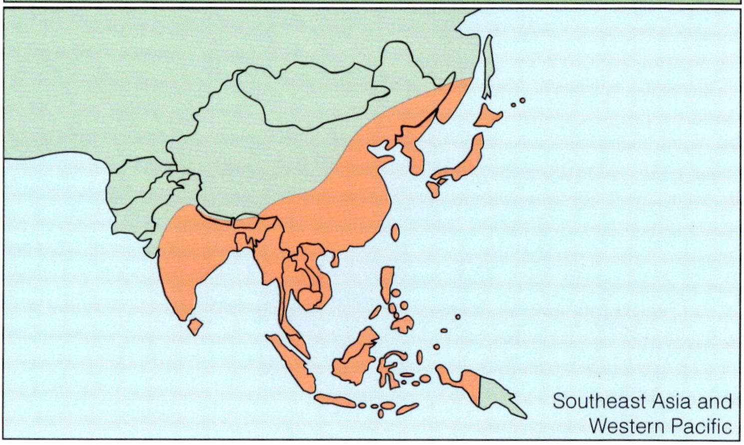

MENINGOCOCCAL MENINGITIS A&C

Transmission: Droplet infection or direct contact with carriers

Risk areas: Worldwide

High risk: Sub-Saharan Africa (especially during the dry season, December to May; *see list overleaf*), northern India, Nepal, Saudi Arabia

Recommendations:
High-risk groups:

- Teachers and health workers intending to work in high-risk areas
- People going to live in high-risk areas and former immigrants returning to visit family and friends in high-risk areas, especially children who may attend local schools
- Those going on prolonged backpacking trips through Africa, Nepal or northern India
- Pilgrims to Mecca during the Hajj: the vaccine must be given at least 10 days before travelling to Saudi Arabia and a certificate of vaccination is needed, which is valid for 3 years; the vaccine is also recommended for all persons staying in Saudi Arabia long term

Vaccination is not recommended for all travellers to these areas because most tourists are at very low risk.

Vaccine: Inactivated polysaccharide capsular vaccine against meningococcal serogroups A and C
Storage: 2–8°C; do not freeze

Schedule:	
Dosage	Adults and children > 18 months 0.5 ml, subcutaneous injection
Primary course	One dose only
Effective	After 15 days
Duration of protection	3–5 years. In children < 5 years, antibody levels decline more rapidly and are unlikely to persist for more than 2 years
Booster	After 3–5 years

Pregnancy: No adverse reactions or harm to the fetus have been reported, but vaccination should be avoided unless a clear indication exists

Children: Safe for children aged less than 18 months, but they respond less well than adults, with little response to the group C polysaccharide in those aged less than 18 months and to group A polysaccharide in those less than 3 months; protection in children aged less than 18 months is of shorter duration

Contraindications: Severe febrile illness, previous severe reaction to vaccine

Side effects:
Local: erythema, pain (10%)
General: rare; transient fever occasionally

Countries considered to be in the African meningitis belt:
Angola, Benin, Burundi, Burkina Faso, Cameroon, Central African Republic, Chad, Djibouti, Eritrea, Ethiopia, Gambia, Ghana, Guinea, Guinea-Bissau, Ivory Coast, Kenya, Liberia, Mali, Mozambique, Niger, Nigeria (north), Rwanda, Somalia, Senegal (south, sub-Saharan), Sierra Leone (north), Sudan, Tanzania, Togo, Uganda, Zambia

POLIO

Transmission: Mainly faecal–oral route, either person-to-person or through contaminated food or water

Risk areas: Many countries worldwide *(see map)*

Recommendations: All individuals worldwide should be vaccinated against polio.

Booster doses are recommended for all travellers to areas where polio is endemic or has been endemic until recently.

Polio appears to have been eradicated from the Americas, so, if vaccination is contraindicated, travellers to these areas should not be immunized.

Vaccines: Live oral vaccine (Sabin)
Storage: SmithKline Beecham, 2–8°C; do not freeze; Evans, 0–4°C

Inactivated polio vaccine (Salk); available on a named-patient basis only for those for whom oral polio vaccine is contraindicated

Schedule:	
Dosage	Adults and children 3 drops orally (live vaccine) or 0.5 ml, subcutaneous injection (inactivated vaccine)
Primary course	Three doses, at 1-month intervals
Effective	After third dose
Duration of protection	10 years
Booster	One dose 10-yearly

Pregnancy: Oral polio vaccine should not be given to pregnant women; if travel to an endemic area cannot be avoided, inactivated polio vaccine can be given

Children: Part of the childhood vaccine schedule: ensure that children are up-to-date with their routine vaccines

Contraindications: Both live oral and inactivated polio vaccines may contain trace elements of penicillin, streptomycin and neomycin; individuals with extreme sensitivity to these antibiotics should not be vaccinated

Acute febrile illness, previous severe reaction to vaccine

For oral polio vaccine, diarrhoea, vomiting and contraindications for live vaccines *(see Live vaccines: guidelines for use)*. Oral polio vaccine should not be used for the sibliings and household contacts of immunosuppressed children; such contacts should be given inactivated polio vaccine

Oral polio vaccine should not be given at the same time as oral typhoid vaccine: a gap of at least 2 weeks is recommended. Other live vaccines can be given at the same time or 3 weeks apart

Side effects: After live polio vaccination, tiny amounts of the vaccine are excreted in the faeces for up to 6 weeks. Rare cases of polio have occurred in recipients of oral polio vaccine and unimmunized contacts; the need for strict personal hygiene must be stressed

Notes:
Routine vaccination started in 1956 in the UK, so many people have received a primary course in childhood. Adults who have never been vaccinated should receive the full primary course.

Global incidence of indigenous polio, 1994

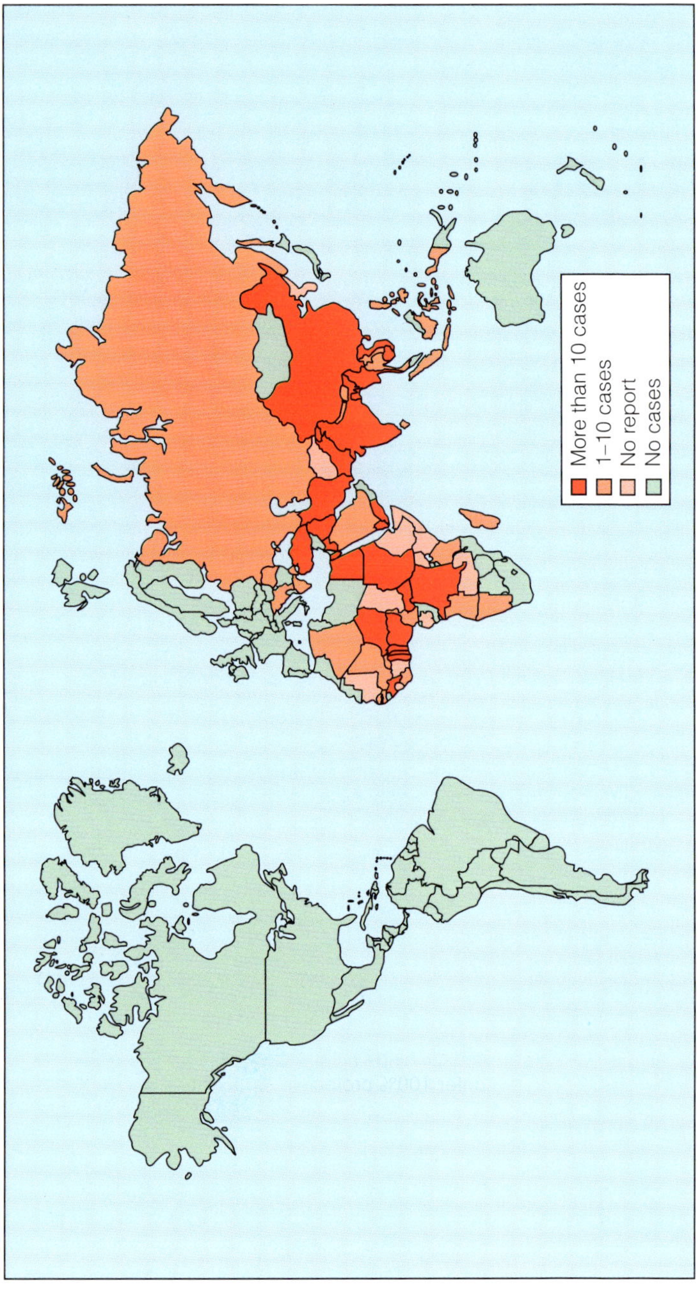

RABIES — PRE-EXPOSURE VACCINATION

Transmission: Bite, scratch or lick from a rabid animal, most often a bite from a rabid dog

Risk areas: Almost worldwide, particularly Thailand, India, South East Asia, Africa, Central and South America

Recommendations: Pre-exposure vaccination is recommended for high-risk travellers going to areas where rabies is present.

High-risk groups:

- Those at risk because of their occupation, such as vets
- Those intending to travel in remote areas where medical help may not be available, especially if likely to be more than 24 h away from a source of vaccine
- Those intending to spend long periods (6 months or more) in developing countries, especially children

Vaccine: Human diploid cell rabies vaccine
Storage: 2–8°C; do not freeze

Schedule — pre-exposure vaccine:	
Dosage:	Adults and children > 1 year 1 ml, subcutaneous injection to deltoid region or 0.1 ml, intradermally (effective but unlicensed application)
Primary course:	Three doses, on days 0, 7 and 28
Effective:	After third dose
Duration of protection:	2–3 years; additional doses of vaccine should be given if exposure to a rabid or suspect animal occurs
Booster	One dose every 2–3 years

Pregnancy: Only give if absolutely essential, although no adverse effects in mother or fetus have been reported

Children: Pre-exposure vaccine not recommended in children aged less than 1 year

Contraindications: Severe febrile illness, previous severe reaction to vaccine

Side effects:
Local: erythema, swelling, pain
General: headache, fever, muscle pain, vomiting, rashes

Notes:

Travellers must seek medical help in the event of a bite. Pre-exposure rabies vaccination does not confer 100% protection, so further doses of vaccine are required.

Travellers who are already taking chloroquine for malaria prophylaxis should be given full 1 ml intramuscular doses of rabies vaccination.

A different schedule is recommended for people who have been bitten by a possibly rabid animal; consult an expert or refer to a suitable source *(see Immunisation against Infectious Diseases [Appendix III])*.

The advantages of pre-exposure vaccinations are twofold: it allows more time to reach medical care because the vaccine is usually effective even if a short delay occurs before additional doses are obtained, and it simplifies the management after a bite because rabies immunoglobulin is not required. Those who have not received pre-exposure vaccination usually need both rabies immunoglobulin and a course of rabies vaccine.

TETANUS

Transmission: Spores in soil and dust, which may be introduced into any wound when the skin is breached

Risk areas: Worldwide

Recommendations: All individuals worldwide should be vaccinated.

Vaccine: Adsorbed toxoid, inactivated vaccine
Storage: 2–8°C; do not freeze

Schedule:	
Dosage	Adults and children > 10 years 0.5 ml, deep subcutaneous injection. Low-dose combined diphtheria–tetanus vaccine if diphtheria also required; tetanus toxoid if diphtheria not required
Primary course	Three doses, at 4-week intervals
Effective	After third dose of primary course
Duration of protection	10 years
Booster	One dose 10-yearly; if five doses have been given before leaving school, only one further booster is needed for travel vaccination

Pregnancy: Safe; all pregnant women should be fully immunized

Children: Included in the childhood vaccine schedule: ensure that children are up-to-date with their routine vaccines

Contraindications: Acute febrile illness unless a tetanus-prone wound is present, previous severe reaction to vaccine

Side effects:
Local: erythema, swelling
General: headache, malaise, myalgia, pyrexia (all uncommon)

Notes:
Hypersensitivity may occur if doses are repeated too frequently.

This schedule is for travellers. In the event of a tetanus-prone wound, consult *Immunisation against Infectious Diseases [Appendix III]* for appropriate management.

TICK-BORNE ENCEPHALITIS

Transmission: Bite from an infected tick

Risk areas: Forested regions of Austria, Germany, Scandinavia, Eastern Europe and western states of the former USSR; high-risk period is from June to September

Recommendations: Individuals who intend walking, camping, or working for prolonged periods in woodlands or forests in Europe in the spring and summer; anyone staying in these areas should take care to avoid tick bites by covering up (wearing long-sleeved shirts and trousers) and using insect repellents.

Vaccine: Inactivated tick-borne encephalitis virus vaccine (unlicensed in UK, available on named-patient basis only)
Storage: 2–8°C; do not freeze

Schedule:	
Dosage	Adults and children > 1 year 0.5 ml, intramuscular injection, preferably to deltoid muscle
Primary course	Three doses; second after 1–3 months, third after 9–12 months
Effective	After second dose
Duration of protection	After second dose, up to 1 year; after third dose, 3 years
Booster	One dose of 0.5 ml can be given after 3 years

Pregnancy: No contraindications during pregnancy or lactation, but it should be avoided unless a clear indication exists

Children: No age limit; should be given to children aged less than 1 year only if actual risk of infection

Contraindications: Severe febrile illness, severe reaction to previous vaccine

Side effects:
Local: erythema, swelling
General: fatigue, limb pain, nausea, headache, lymphadenopathy

TUBERCULOSIS

Transmission: Droplet infection and rarely by infected dairy products

Risk areas: Worldwide but more common in developing countries

Recommendations: High-risk travellers should receive vaccination if they have a negative reading on the Mantoux (Heaf) test and they have never had a BCG.

High-risk groups:

- Health workers and teachers who will be working in developing countries
- Infants and children who will be living in developing countries
- Travellers who will be living under local conditions in developing countries for several months or more

NOTE: Repeat vaccination is not recommended for people who have previously received BCG, including those who have had BCG and now have a negative Mantoux test.

A Mantoux (or Heaf) tuberculin skin test should be carried out before administration of BCG for all travellers aged more than 3 months. If the test is negative, BCG may be given.

The Mantoux test is read after 48–72 h. Live vaccines may suppress the test and should not be given until after the test has been read.

Skin induration	Heaf grade	Action required
0–4	0–1	BCG can be given
5–14	2	BCG not required
> 15	3–4	Refer for medical attention

Vaccine: Live attenuated intradermal BCG (bacille Calmette-Guérin) vaccine
Storage: 2–8°C; do not freeze

Schedule:	
Dosage	Adults and children > 3 months 0.1 ml, babies < 3 months 0.05 ml; strict intradermal injection to deltoid region
Primary course	One dose only
Effective	After 6–8 weeks
Duration of protection	At least 15 years (according to data from studies in UK schoolchildren)
Booster	Not recommended

Pregnancy: Do not give

Children: Safe; can be given from birth

Contraindications: Contraindications to live vaccines *(see Live vaccines: guidelines for use)*, acute febrile illness, HIV infection, positive tuberculin test, generalized septic skin conditions, pregnancy

VACCINE GUIDELINES

Side effects:
Local: severe injection-site reactions, large ulcers and abscesses (usually due to faulty injection technique)
General: occasionally lymphadenitis, rarely widespread dissemination of injected organisms

Notes:
BCG can be given at the same time as oral polio vaccine or inactivated vaccines given into the opposite limb.

Allow 3 weeks or more between giving BCG and other live vaccines.

TYPHOID

Transmission: Faecal–oral route, usually through contaminated food and water

Risk areas: Worldwide, predominantly in countries where food and water are liable to faecal contamination, especially Asia, Africa and South and Central America

Recommendations: The incidence of travellers contracting typhoid is low, so we do not recommend routine vaccination for all travellers.

Advice about eating and drinking safely must be stressed.

Most new typhoid cases in the UK are imported, mainly from the Indian subcontinent, many of these occurring in the families of former immigrants who have been visiting relatives and friends.

High-risk groups:

- Travellers who will be living under local conditions in developing countries and those on prolonged trips
- Former immigrants and their families who are returning to visit relatives in developing countries
- All travellers to the Indian subcontinent, unless they will be staying for only a few days in a city and will be living and eating in good conditions

Vaccines: Inactivated and live typhoid vaccines are available, all about 70% effective

- Inactivated polysaccharide antigen vaccine
- Monovalent whole-cell typhoid vaccine *(currently unavailable in the UK)*
- Live oral Ty21a typhoid vaccine

Storage: 2–8°C; do not freeze

Inactivated polysaccharide vaccine

Schedule:	
Dosage	Adults and children > 18 months 0.5 ml, subcutaneous injection
Primary course	One dose
Effective	After 10 days
Duration of protection	3 years
Booster	Every 3 years if at risk (or use booster dose of typhoid monovalent vaccine)

Pregnancy: Not recommended unless the patient is considered to be at high risk of contracting typhoid; consult a specialist

Children: Ineffective in children aged less than 18 months; extra care with food, water and hygiene should be advised

Contraindications: Febrile illness, previous severe reaction to vaccine

Side effects:

Local: mild pain, erythema
General: systemic reactions unusual, transient malaise and pyrexia reported

VACCINE GUIDELINES

Notes:

Recommended for travellers who have never been vaccinated against typhoid because of the low incidence of side effects.

When available, monovalent typhoid vaccine can be used for booster doses.

Typhoid monovalent whole-cell vaccine *(currently unavailable in the UK)*

Schedule:	
Dosage	Adults and children > 10 years 0.5 ml, children 1–10 years 0.25 ml, deep subcutaneous injection
Primary course	Two doses, 1 month apart
Effective	After 10 days
Duration of protection	3 years
Booster	Every 3 years, 0.1 ml intradermal injection

Pregnancy: Not recommended unless the patient is considered to be at high risk of contracting typhoid; consult a specialist

Children: Not recommended for children aged less than 12 months; extra care with food, water and hygeine should be advised

Contraindications: Febrile illness, previous severe reaction to vaccine

Side effects:

Local: often redness, swelling, pain, tenderness, less severe after intradermal injection

General: malaise, fever, nausea, headache

Oral Ty21a typhoid vaccine

Schedule:	
Dosage	Adults and children > 6 years, 1 capsule
Primary course	Three doses on alternate days (days 0, 2 and 4)
Effective	7–10 days after final dose
Duration of protection	1 year
Booster	Annually, full 3-dose course

Pregnancy: Should not be given

Children: Unsuitable for children aged less than 6 years because capsule must be swallowed whole

Contraindications: Contraindications to live vaccines *(see Live vaccines: guidelines for use)*, should not be given to those taking antibiotics

Febrile illness, previous severe reaction to vaccine

In those taking mefloquine, at least 12 h should elapse between taking the mefloquine and the oral typhoid vaccine (Ty21a)

A gap of at least 2 weeks is advised between giving the oral polio vaccine and oral typhoid vaccine (Ty21a); other live vaccines can be given at the same time or 3 weeks apart

Side effects:

General: transient gastrointestinal symptoms (possibly)

Notes:

Recommended for travellers who have never been vaccinated against typhoid because of the low incidence of side effects.

YELLOW FEVER

Transmission: Mosquito bites

Risk areas: Tropical Africa, South America *(see map)*

Recommendations: Strongly recommended for travel to all countries in the endemic zone, even if some countries do not require evidence of vaccination on entry and have not officially reported the disease.

Vaccine: Live attenuated yellow fever vaccine
Storage: 2–8°C, do not freeze

Schedule:	
Dosage	Adults and children > 9 months 0.5 ml, deep subcutaneous injection
Primary course	One dose only
Effective	After 10 days
Duration of protection	10 years
Booster	10-yearly

Pregnancy: Not recommended unless travel to a high-risk area cannot be avoided or postponed; a specialist should be consulted

Children: Not recommended in children aged less than 9 months when vaccination carries a very small risk of encephalitis and a specialist should be consulted; travel to high-risk areas should be avoided if possible

Contraindications: Contraindications to live vaccines *(see Live vaccines: guidelines for use)*, severe febrile illness, previous anaphylactic reaction to egg

Side effects:
Local: mild pain
General: headache, myalgia, low-grade fever 5–10 days after vaccination (5–10%); severe reactions rare

Notes:
Other live vaccines can be given at the same time or 3 weeks apart.

Vaccination must take place in a designated Yellow Fever centre *(see Health Information for Overseas Travel [Appendix III])* and the international yellow fever certificate be given, which should be kept with the passport at all times. The certificate becomes valid 10 days after vaccination and lasts for 10 years. If a person is revaccinated before the end of this period, the validity is extended for a further 10 years from the date of revaccination. If the revaccination is recorded on a new certificate, travellers are advised to retain the old certificate for 10 days until the new certificate becomes valid.

Some countries require evidence of vaccination. This mainly applies to travellers who are arriving from countries with infected areas, but in certain countries it can apply to all travellers or to all travellers arriving from Africa or South America. Country requirements are given in the recommended literature *(see International Travel and Health* and *Health Information for Overseas Travel [Appendix III])*. Tourists from the UK travelling only to Asia direct from the UK do not need the yellow fever vaccine.

If an individual should not be vaccinated on medical grounds and a certificate is required for entry, an exemption certificate can be provided by a physician. Travel to high-risk areas should be avoided.

Countries considered to be in the yellow fever zone:

Africa: Angola, Benin, Burkina Faso, Burundi, Cameroon, Central African Republic, Chad, Congo, Equatorial Guinea, Ethiopia, Gabon, Gambia, Ghana, Guinea, Guinea-Bissau, Ivory Coast, Kenya, Liberia, Mali, Niger, Nigeria, Rwanda, Sao Tome & Principe, Senegal, Sierra Leone, Somalia, Sudan, Tanzania, Togo, Uganda, Zaire, Zambia

South America: Bolivia, Brazil, Colombia, Ecuador, French Guiana, Guyana, Panama, Peru, Suriname, Venezuela

Yellow fever endemic zone

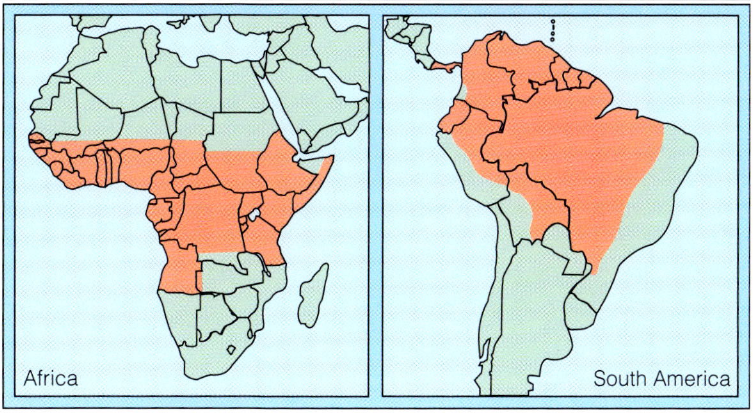

APPENDIX III: FURTHER STUDY

Suggested reading

Anonymous: *The Red Book — Statement of fees and allowances payable to general medical practitioners in England and Wales.* London: NHS Publications; 1990.

Anonymous: *British National Formulary.* London: British Medical Association and Royal Pharmaceutical Society of Great Britain; 1996 (updated every 6 months).

Department of Health: *Health Information for Overseas Travel.* London: HMSO; 1995.

Department of Health: *Immunisation against Infectious Disease.* London: HMSO; 1992.

Dudgeon JA, Cutting WAM: *Immunisation, Principles and Practice.* London: Chapman and Hall; 1991.

Anonymous: *International Travel and Health. Vaccination Requirements and Health Advice.* Geneva: World Health Organization; 1996.

Bell D: *Lecture Notes on Tropical Medicine*, edn 4. Oxford: Blackwell Science; 1995.

Bradley DJ, Warhurst DC: **Malaria prophylaxis guidelines for travellers from Britain**. *BMJ* 1995, **310**:709–714.

Bradley DJ: **Prophylaxis against malaria for travellers from the United Kingdom**. *BMJ* 1993, **306**:1247–1252.

Cook GC: **Manson's Tropical Diseases,** edn 20**.** London: WB Saunders; 1995.

Courses

Liverpool School of Tropical Medicine
Pembroke Place, Liverpool LS 5QA
Runs 2–3 travel health days a year for nurses and general practitioners

RCN Travel Health Special Interest Group
Royal College of Nurses, 20 Cavendish Square, London W1M 0AB
Open to all nurses, runs 2–3 study days a year in different regions of the UK

Diploma in Travel Medicine, validated by Glasgow University
Ruchill Hospital, Glasgow G20 9NB, Tel 0141 946 7120
12-month course with distant-learning modules open to health professionals working in travel-related areas

APPENDIX IV: USEFUL ADDRESSES

Liverpool School of Tropical Medicine
Pembroke Place, Liverpool L3 5QA, Tel 0151 708 9393
Enquiries from health-care professionals only

The Scottish Centre for Infection and Environmental Health
Ruchill Hospital,Glasgow G20 9NB, Tel 0141 946 7120
Enquiries from health-care professionals only

TRAVAX
Tel 0141 946 7120 extn 1510
Provided by the Scottish Centre for Infection and Environmental Health, this is a computerized database containing information about health risks in different countries, with recommendations about vaccinations and malaria prophylaxis. Can be accessed on-line, using a computer with viewdata software and modem, free of charge for practitioners

Department of Infection and Tropical Medicine
Birmingham Heartlands Hospital, Birmingham B9 5ST
Tel 0121 766 6611 extn 4403, 4382 or 4535
Enquiries from health-care professionals only

Public Health Laboratory Service
Communicable Disease Surveillance Centre Travel Unit
61 Colindale Avenue, London NW9 5EQ, Tel 0181 200 6868
Enquiries from health-care professionals only

Public Health Laboratory Service Malaria Reference Laboratory
London School of Hygiene and Tropical Medicine
Keppel Street, London WC1E 7HT
24-h recorded message 0800 600 350 (currently 39p/min cheap rate, 49p/min all other times)
Advice about malaria prevention
Tel 0171 927 2437
Advice on specific patients and other queries from health-care professionals only

Hospital for Tropical Diseases Travel Clinic
4 St Pancras Way, London NW1 0PE, Tel 0171 388 0000
Enquiries from health-care professionals only

Lister Unit for Infection and Tropical Medicine
Northwick Park Hospital, Harrow, Middlesex HA1 3UJ
Tel 0181 869 2831 or 2833
Enquiries from health-care professionals only

HEF 2, Department of Health
Skipton House, 80 London Road, London SE1 6LW
Only designated centres can give yellow fever vaccine and the certificate of vaccination; practitioners wishing to apply for designation should write to the address above

International Society of Travel Medicine
PO Box 871089, Stone Mountain, GA30087-0028, USA

APPENDIX V: INFORMATION FOR TRAVELLERS

Liverpool School of Tropical Medicine — Travel Health Advice Line
Tel 0891 172 111 (currently 39p/min cheap rate, 49p/min at all other times)
24 h recorded message gives country specific information on immunization, malaria prophylaxis and general health advice; travel clinic open Monday to Friday 13.00 to 16.00

MASTA
Keppel Street, London, WC1E 7HT
Tel 0891 224 100 (currently 39p/min cheap rate, 49p/min at all other times)
Supplies written information for travellers

Foreign and Commonwealth Office
Tel 0171 270 4129
Public 'Advice to Travellers' enquiry line on safety abroad

Department of Health:*Health Advice for Travellers.* London: HMSO; 1995.
Free from the Department of Health, Tel 0800 555 777
Leaflet containing basic health advice including avoiding insect bites, accidents, sun, food and water, and the E-111 form

Ryan R: *Stay Healthy Abroad.* London: Health Education Authority; 1995.
Pre-travel health advice for all travellers, especially backpackers and long-term travellers

Dawood R: *Traveller's Health, How to Stay Healthy Abroad.* Oxford: Oxford University Press; 1992.
Pre-travel and during-travel health advice; useful for people who will be spending long periods in developing countries

Anonymous: *The Traveller's Handbook.* London: Wexas Ltd; 1994.
General travel advice, with specific sections on health issues and travellers with special needs

British Diabetic Association
10 Queen Anne Street, London W1M 0BD, Tel 0171 323 1531
Specific information on diabetes and travel; country-specific travel guides available

Blood Care Foundation
16 Lonsdale Gardens, Tunbridge Wells, Kent TN1 1NU
A charitable organization that couriers screened blood to members if a transfusion is required. Fees start from £7.50 for 1 month's membership; enquiries should be directed through MASTA, tel 0113 239 1700

INDEX

- accidents, avoiding 1, 28
- allergies to vaccines 4, 60
- analgesics 18, 23
- antibiotics 23
  - and contraceptives 27
  - for diarrhoea 25
- antihistamine tablets 23
- antipyretics 18, 23
- antiseptic cream 23

- BCG vaccine 3, 79–80
  - and children 19, 79
  - and HIV 5
  - and pregnancy 17, 79
  - indications by country 35–59
- bilharzia *see* schistosomiasis
- bites 30
- breast-feeding and malaria 14, 18

- children 2, 18–20
  - vaccinations 19, 60–85
- chloroquine for malaria prophylaxis 10, 12
  - and contraceptives 27
  - in children 20
- cholera 61
  - and diarrhoea 24
  - vaccination 61
    - and children 61
    - and pregnancy 61
- ciprofloxacin for diarrhoea 25
- contraception 27

- dengue fever 29
- developing countries, travellers living in 2
- diabetes mellitus 22
- diarrhoea 24–25
  - and contraceptives 27
  - in the returned traveller 32
- diphtheria 62–63
  - vaccine 19, 62
    - in children 62
    - indications by country 35–59
    - in pregnancy 62
- diphtheria–tetanus vaccine 3, 4
- doxycycline
  - and contraceptives 27
  - for malaria prophylaxis 14

- encephalitis
- epilepsy and malaria prophylaxis 14

- falciparum malaria 7
- fever in the returned traveller 32
- first-aid kits 23
- flying 23, 30–31

- H_2 receptor antagonists 21
- halofantrine 16
- health problems, pre-existing 2, 21
- heart disease 21
- heat 28–29
- hepatitis A 4, 64–65
  - and diarrhoea 24
  - and former immigrants 21
  - and HIV 6
  - and pregnancy 17, 64
  - protection against 3, 64
  - vaccine 64
    - and children 19, 64
    - claiming for 6
    - indications by country 35–59
- hepatitis B 25, 66–67
  - vaccine 66
    - and children 19, 66
    - and pregnancy 66
    - claiming for 6
    - indications by country 35–59
- Hib vaccine 19
- HIV infection 22, 25–27
  - and vaccination 4, 5–6
  - distribution 26
- hypersensitivity reactions to vaccines 4, 60

- illness in the returned traveller 32–33
- immigrants, former 2, 20–21
  - and malaria prophylaxis 14
- immunoglobulin, human normal, for hepatitis A protection 3, 65
  - and children 65
  - and pregnancy 17, 65
- immunosuppression and vaccination 4, 5

- Japanese encephalitis 29, 68–70
  - vaccination 68
    - and children 68
    - and pregnancy 68
    - indications by country 35–59

- loperamide for diarrhoea 25

- malaria 7–16, 29
  - and breast-feeding 14
  - and children 19
  - and former immigrants 14
  - and pregnancy 14, 18
  - and special cases 14–15
  - and the returned traveller 32
  - diagnosis 7
  - drug resistance 9, 15
  - epidemiology 8
  - incidence 7
  - prevention 1, 7, 9–14
    - after return 32
  - prophylaxis 9–10
    - adverse reactions 11
    - and children 20
    - and pregnancy 18
    - drugs 10
    - effectiveness 11
    - indications by country 34–59

malaria (*continued*)
risk of infection 7, 11
by country 34–59
standby treatment 15–16
transmission 7, 29
measles vaccine 3
medical kits 23
mefloquine
and contraceptives 27
prophylaxis for malaria 13
in children 20
standby treatment for malaria 16
meningitis, meningococcal A&C 71–72
vaccine 71
and children 71
and pregnancy 71
claiming for 6
indications by country 35, 59
MMR vaccine 3, 19
and pregnancy 17
mosquitoes 9, 29

paracetamol 18, 23
pertussis vaccination 19
pilots and malaria prophylaxis 15
polio 73–74
and diarrhoea 24
vaccines 3, 19, 73
and children 73
and HIV 5
and pregnancy 17, 73
claiming for 6
indications by country 35–59
pregnancy 2, 4, 5, 17–18
and flying 31
and malaria 17–18
and vaccines 17, 60–85
proguanil for malaria prophylaxis 10, 12
and contraceptives 27
in children 20
pyrimethamine–sulfadoxine for malaria standby treatment 16

quinine for malaria standby treatment 16

rabies 30, 75–76
vaccine 75
and children 75
and pregnancy 17, 75
indications by country 35–59
rehydration 18, 23, 24
renal failure and malaria prophylaxis 15
risk assessment 1–2

schistosomiasis 30
in the returned traveller 32
screening asymptomatic returned travellers 33
sexually transmitted diseases, avoiding 1, 25
sleeping sickness 29
swimming accidents, advice for travellers 28

tetanus 77
vaccine 4, 19, 77
and children 77
and pregnancy 77
claiming for 6
indications by country 35–59
tetracycline for malaria standby treatment 16
tick-borne encephalitis 78
vaccine 78
and children 78
and pregnancy 78
tuberculosis 79–80
typhoid 81–83
and diarrhoea 24
vaccine 3, 5, 81–83
and children 19, 81, 82
and HIV 5
and pregnancy 17, 81, 82
claiming for 6
indications by country 35–59

vaccines 1, 3–6 *see also specific disorders*
and children 19
and HIV 6
and pregnancy 17
claiming for 6
contraindications 4–5
guidelines 5, 60–85
inactivated 3
live 3
indications by country 34–59
routes of administration 4
schedules 3–4

water sterilization, advice for travellers 25
worms 29, 30

yellow fever 84–85
vaccine 3, 84–85
and children 19, 84
and HIV 5
and pregnancy 17, 84
indications by country 35–59